Adane Nega Tarekegn
Alemu Kumilachew Tegegne

A Simple Guide to Computer Maintenance and Troubleshooting

Adane Nega Tarekegn
Alemu Kumilachew Tegegne

A Simple Guide to Computer Maintenance and Troubleshooting

LAP LAMBERT Academic Publishing

Impressum / Imprint
Bibliografische Information der Deutschen Nationalbibliothek: Die Deutsche Nationalbibliothek verzeichnet diese Publikation in der Deutschen Nationalbibliografie; detaillierte bibliografische Daten sind im Internet über http://dnb.d-nb.de abrufbar.
Alle in diesem Buch genannten Marken und Produktnamen unterliegen warenzeichen-, marken- oder patentrechtlichem Schutz bzw. sind Warenzeichen oder eingetragene Warenzeichen der jeweiligen Inhaber. Die Wiedergabe von Marken, Produktnamen, Gebrauchsnamen, Handelsnamen, Warenbezeichnungen u.s.w. in diesem Werk berechtigt auch ohne besondere Kennzeichnung nicht zu der Annahme, dass solche Namen im Sinne der Warenzeichen- und Markenschutzgesetzgebung als frei zu betrachten wären und daher von jedermann benutzt werden dürften.

Bibliographic information published by the Deutsche Nationalbibliothek: The Deutsche Nationalbibliothek lists this publication in the Deutsche Nationalbibliografie; detailed bibliographic data are available in the Internet at http://dnb.d-nb.de.
Any brand names and product names mentioned in this book are subject to trademark, brand or patent protection and are trademarks or registered trademarks of their respective holders. The use of brand names, product names, common names, trade names, product descriptions etc. even without a particular marking in this work is in no way to be construed to mean that such names may be regarded as unrestricted in respect of trademark and brand protection legislation and could thus be used by anyone.

Coverbild / Cover image: www.ingimage.com

Verlag / Publisher:
LAP LAMBERT Academic Publishing
ist ein Imprint der / is a trademark of
OmniScriptum GmbH & Co. KG
Bahnhofstraße 28, 66111 Saarbrücken, Deutschland / Germany
Email: info@lap-publishing.com

Herstellung: siehe letzte Seite /
Printed at: see last page
ISBN: 978-3-659-69929-0

Zugl. / Approved by: Bahir Dar,Bahir Dar University,2015

A Simple Guide to

Computer Maintenance and Troubleshooting

Main author: Adane Nega Tarekegn

Co-author: Alemu Kumilachew Tegegnie

July 2015

Acknowledgement

First of all, we would like to give a special gratitude to the gracious God who provided us everything to finish this book.

We would like to thank Mr. Workineh Checkol for her drive and support to complete this book and who also worked as editor of this book. His excellent practical tips and suggestions really help to keep the book concise and up to date. Second, we appreciate Yordanos G/Michael for her valuable input, comments and inspiration to produce this book. Students and instructors in computer maintenance and repair course at Bahir Dar Institute of Technology have used drafts of this book and provided us with useful comments that led to the improvement of the presentation of the material in the book.

Finally, we would like to thank many people for their kindness and assistance during the production of this book. We truly appreciate the support of the people at Bahir Dar University.

Preface

This book contains various procedures and guidelines for maintaining, troubleshooting and repairing personal computer problems. It offers the most common problem causes and solutions of current operating systems, processors, memory, hard drives, and other components. The book concentrates on practical and hands-on solutions that can help users to fix computer problems by themselves, without calling an experienced PC technician. Regardless of your level of experience, this is a good resource for anyone who wants to repair a computer or is considering a career in the computer repair business.

Many different computer related problems that one may face in the day to day activities are analyzed and solved in this book. This book is also written based on authors' long term teaching and practical experiences. It pays special attention to most common hardware and software problems, installation of windows 8/7/XP, BIOS Setup Configuration, data backup and recovery and PC diagnostic tools and procedures.

This book is intended for people who have basic computer knowledge and working on their computers and for people who want to understand what goes on inside a computer. Moreover, the book can also be used as a teaching material for instructors and as reference for college students.

Chapter 1 starts with a brief explanation of hardware components and their functions in computer system. Chapter 2 focuses of disassembling and assembling a computer. This chapter also introduces the basic tools and safety precautions that can be applied in the process of disassembling and assembling a PC. Chapter 3 covers about BIOS and BIOS configuration. Chapter 4 introduces software. This chapter contains discussion of operating systems, operating system installation and common window problems and solutions. Chapter 5 presents common hardware problems and solutions. Chapter 6 covers issues related to protecting and securing computer from unauthorized access. Chapter 7 is dedicated to a study about window built-in troubleshooting tools. Chapter 8 shows the main procedures in the diagnosis and troubleshooting of computer problems. Chapter 9 is all about the data backup and recovery mechanisms. Chapter 10 contains a collection common problems and possible solutions that will guide any one as quick reference.

Table of Contents

Chapter One

Introduction to Computer Hardware

1.1. Overview of computers

A computer is a machine that processes data; that is, it takes information (data) from the user and does something with it (processes it). Then it takes that processed information and outputs it, or puts it back out to you in a way you can understand. The output may be to the screen for you to view or to paper (hard copy) for you to hold in your hands or onto a disk or tape that you can store in a safe place. Basically, then, a computer does these three things:

- ✓ Accepts input
- ✓ Processes data
- ✓ Outputs information

Parts of computer

A computer system has two major parts: - hardware and software.

- ✓ **Hardware** refers to the computer's physical components, such as the monitor, keyboard, motherboard, and hard drive.
- ✓ **Software** refers to the set of instructions that directs the hardware to accomplish a task.

PC hardware components

PC hardware components can be classified as **internal and external** to the system unit.

1.2. Internal Components

Internal components of a PC include:

1

✓ Microprocessor

✓ Motherboard

✓ Storage devices

✓ Expansion cards

✓ Chipsets and controllers

✓ Power supply

1.2.1. Microprocessor

The **brain or engine** of the PC is the processor, sometimes called microprocessor or central processing unit (CPU). The CPU performs the system's calculating and processing. The processor is often the most important component in the system.

Fig.1.1 Central processing unit (CPU)

Microprocessor Speeds

Processor speed or clock speed is the frequency with which a processor executes instructions. CPU speed is measured in Hertz (Hz). Hertz is the number of cycles per second. 1Hz=1cycle per second. Larger units are KHz (Kilo Hertz), MHz (Mega Hertz), GHz (Giga Hertz), etc.

1 KHz = 1000 Hz

1 MHz = 1000 KHz

1 GHz = 1000MHZ

Current CPUs are as fast as 3-4GHz (3-4 billion cycles per second). Generally speaking, the higher the GHz value, the faster the PC.

How do you know speed of the processor in your computer?

You can know your computer's processor speed on window 7 using one of the following steps

Right click on computer icon →properties

Or

Start →programs →accessories →system tools →system information

Or

Start →run→type *msinfo32*→ press Enter

Or

Start →run→type *dxdiag*→ press Enter

Types of processors

The processor installed on a motherboard is the primary component that determines the computing power of the system. The two major manufacturers of processors are Intel (www.intel.com) and AMD (www.amd.com). From manufacturer's perspective processors can be categorized as INTEL or AMD processors.

Intel processors

Intel's current families of processors for the desktop include the following major groups:

✓ Core

✓ Pentium

✓ Celeron

Core family

The most common Core family processors include : Core i7, Core i5 and Core i3

Pentium family

The most common Pentium family processors include : Pentium Dual-Core, Pentium D, Pentium M and Pentium 4.

Celeron family

The most common celeron family processors include the following: Celeron, Celeron D and Celeron M.

AMD processors

AMD (Advanced Micro Devices) are popular in the game and hobbyist markets, and are generally less expensive than comparable Intel processors. AMD processors use different sockets than do Intel processors, so the motherboard must be designed for one manufacturer's processor or the other, but not both. Many motherboard manufacturers offer two comparable motherboards—one for an Intel processor and one for an AMD processor. The current AMD processor families are: - Phenom, Athlon, Sempron and Turion

Processor Cooling

The processor produces heat, and, if it gets overheated, it can become damaged and unstable. If the entire system overheats, other sensitive electronic components can also be damaged. Devices that are used to cool a system include: - CPU fans, heat sinks, Dust-preventing tools and so on.

A heat sink is a metallic device that sits directly on the CPU, drawing heat away from the chip into its cooler, aluminum, and fin-like structure.

The CPU fan attaches to the heat sink, pulling air through the fins. By dissipating heat drawn into the heat sink, the CPU fan indirectly cools the processor.

Dealing with dust - dust is not good for a PC because it insulates PC parts like a blanket, which can cause them to overheat. Dust inside fans can jam fans, and fans not working can cause a system to overheat. Therefore, ridding the PC of dust is an important part of keeping a system cool and should be done as part of a regular preventive maintenance plan, at least twice a year.

Installing a Pentium 4 processor in socket 478

The following are the steps used for installing Pentium 4 processor

- ➤ Power off the system
- ➤ Lift the ZIF socket lever
- ➤ Place the processor on the socket so that the corner marked with a triangle is aligned with the connection of the lever to the socket
- ➤ installing the heat sink fan on top
- ➤ Connect the power cord from the processor fan to the power connection on the mother board next to the cooler

1.2.2. Motherboard

The spine of the computer is the motherboard, also called the main board or the system board. This is the olive green or brown circuit board that lines the bottom of the computer. It is the most important component in the computer because it connects all the other components of a PC together. Motherboard is the main circuit board in the computer where everything comes together such as to plug in processor, memory, cache, video card, sound card, NIC, modem card, etc. Because all devices must communicate with the CPU installed on the motherboard, all devices in a computer are either installed directly on the motherboard, directly linked to it by a cable connected to a port on the motherboard, or indirectly linked to it by expansion cards. A device that is not installed directly on the motherboard is called a peripheral device.

Motherboard Form factor

The terms basically describe the shape and size of the motherboards, as well as the layout of the components on the board. The case and power supply must then match the type of motherboard you have chosen.

There are primarily two types of motherboards

- **AT motherboard**
- **ATX motherboard**

AT motherboards

- Older, and not commonly used now days
- Full AT is 12" wide x 13.8" deep
- Baby AT is 8.57" wide x 13.04" deep.
- AT has 5-pin large keyboard connector

ATX motherboards

- Full-ATX is 12" wide x 9.6" deep
- Mini-ATX is 11.2" wide x 8.2" deep.
- ATX has 6-pin mini keyboard connector

Motherboard and its constituent components

Now that you understand the motherboard's form factors, it's time to look at the components found on the motherboard and their locations relative to each other. A typical ATX PC motherboard with constituent components is given below:

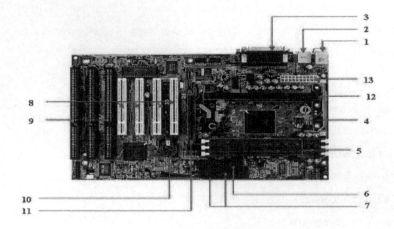

Fig.1.2 Typical ATX motherboard Diagram

The important constituent components of an ATX Motherboard are given below:

1. **Mouse & keyboard**
2. **USB**
3. **Parallel port**
4. **CPU Chip**
5. **RAM slots**
6. **Floppy controller**
7. **IDE controller**

8. **PCI slot**
9. **ISA slot**
10. **CMOS Battery**
11. **AGP slot**
12. **CPU slot**
13. **Power supply plug in**

1. **Mouse & keyboard:** Keyboard Connectors are two types basically. All PCs have a Key board port connected directly to the motherboard. The oldest, but still quite common type, is a special DIN, and most PCs until recently retained this style connector. The AT-style keyboard connector is quickly disappearing, being replaced by the

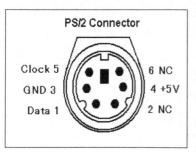

smaller mini DIN PS/2-style keyboard connector. You can use an AT-style keyboard with a PS/2-style socket (or the other way around) by using a converter. Although the AT connector is unique in PCs, the PS/2-style mini-DIN is also used in more modern PCs for the mouse. Fortunately, most PCs that use the mini-DIN for both the keyboard and mouse clearly mark each mini-DIN socket as to its correct use. Some keyboards have a USB connection, but these are fairly rare compared to the PS/2 connection keyboards.

2. **USB (Universal serial bus):** USB is the General-purpose connection for PC. You can find USB versions of many different devices, such as mice, keyboards, scanners, cameras, and even printers. a USB connector's distinctive rectangular shape makes it easily recognizable. USB has a number of features that makes it particularly popular on PCs. First, USB devices are hot swappable. You can insert or remove them without restarting your system.

3. **Parallel port:** Most printers use a special connector called a parallel port. Parallel port carry data on more than one wire, as opposed to the serial port, which uses only one wire. Parallel ports use a 25-pin female DB

connector. Parallel ports are directly supported by the motherboard through a direct connection or through a dangle.

4. **CPU Chip:** The *central processing unit,* also called the *microprocessor* performs all the calculations that take place inside a pc. CPUs come in Variety of shapes and sizes. Modern CPUs generate a lot of heat and thus require a cooling fan or heat sink. The cooling device (such as a cooling fan) is removable, although some CPU manufactures sell the CPU with a fan permanently attached.

5. **RAM slots:** Random-Access Memory (RAM) stores programs and data currently being used by the CPU. RAM is measured in units called bytes. RAM has been packaged in many different ways. The most current package is called a 168-pin DIMM (Dual Inline Memory module).

6. **Floppy controller:** The floppy drive connects to the computer via a 34-pin *ribbon cable,* which in turn connects to the motherboard. A *floppy controller* is one that is used to control the floppy drive.

7. **IDE controller:** Industry standards define two common types of hard drives: EIDE and SCSI. Majority of the PCs use EIDE drives. SCSI drives show up in high end PCs such as network servers or graphical workstations. The EIDE drive connects to the hard drive via a 2-inch-wide, 40-pin ribbon cable, which in turn connects to the motherboard. *IDE controller* is responsible for controlling the hard drive.

8. **PCI slot:** Intel introduced the *Peripheral component interconnect* bus protocol. The PCI bus is used to connect I/O devices (such as NIC or RAID controllers) to the main logic of the computer. PCI bus has replaced the ISA bus.

9. **ISA slot:** (Industry Standard Architecture) It is the standard architecture of the Expansion bus. Motherboard may contain some slots to connect ISA compatible cards.

10. **CMOS Battery:** To provide CMOS with the power when the computer is turned off all motherboards comes with a battery. These batteries mount on the motherboard in one of three ways: the obsolete external battery, the most common onboard battery, and built-in battery.

11. **AGP slot:** If you have a modern motherboard, you will almost certainly notice a single connector that looks like a PCI slot, but is slightly shorter and usually brown. You also probably have a video card inserted into this slot. This is an Advanced Graphics Port (AGP) slot.

12. **CPU slot:** To install the CPU, just slide it straight down into the slot. Special notches in the slot make it impossible to install them incorrectly. So remember if it does not go easily, it is probably not correct. Be sure to plug in the CPU fan's power.

13. **Power supply plug in:** The Power supply, as its name implies, provides the necessary electrical power to make the pc operate. The power supply takes standard 110-V AC power and converts into +/-12-Volt, +/-5-Volt, and 3.3-Volt DC power.

1.2.3. Buses and expansion slots

A bus is a pathway on the motherboard that enables the components to communicate with the CPU. Every expansion card, whether it is a video adapter, modem, or network interface card, is designed to communicate with the motherboard and CPU over a single communications and interface standard that is called a bus. Here are the PC bus structures that have been the most popular over the years:

- ISA
- PCI
- PCI Express (PCIe)
- AGP

ISA (Industry Standard Architecture) Expansion Slots

The ISA expansion bus is now generally obsolete, but most motherboards still have at least one ISA slot to provide backward compatibility for older hardware. You can still buy ISA expansion cards, but they are becoming hard to find. On most motherboards, the ISA bus slots are 16-bit that will also support 8-bit cards. On the motherboard, ISA slots are typically black. ISA was used to add modems, network adapters, and sound cards in to the motherboard.

PCI (Peripheral Component Interconnect) expansion slot

Most computers made today contain primarily Peripheral Component Interconnect (PCI) slots. They are easily recognizable, because they are short (around 3 inches long) and usually white. PCI slots can usually be found in any computer that has a Pentium-class processor or higher. PCI buses have been improved several times; there are currently three major categories and within each category, several variations of PCI; Conventional PCI, PCI-X and PCI express.

Conventional PCI

The first PCI bus had a 32-bit data path, supplied 5 V of power to an expansion card, and operated at 33 MHz. It was the first bus that allowed expansion cards to run in sync with the CPU. PCI Version 2.x introduced the

64-bit, 3.3-V PCI slot, doubling data throughput of the bus. Because a card can be damaged if installed in the wrong voltage slot, a notch in a PCI slot distinguishes between a 5-V slot and a 3.3-V slot. A Universal PCI card can use either a 3.3-V or 5-V slot and contains both notches.

PCI Express

PCI Express (PCIe) uses an altogether different architectural design than conventional PCI and PCI-X; PCIe is not backward compatible with either. PCI Express will ultimately replace both these buses as well as the AGP bus; although it is expected PCI Express will coexist with conventional PCI for some time to come. Whereas PCI uses a 32-bit or 64-bit parallel bus, PCI Express uses a serial bus, which is faster than a parallel bus because it transmits data in packets similar to how an Ethernet network, USB, and FireWire transmit data.

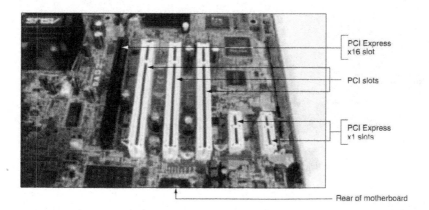

Figure 1.3: Three PCI Express slots and three PCI slots on a motherboard

The AGP buses

Motherboard video slots and video cards used the Accelerated Graphics Port (AGP) standards for many years, but AGP has mostly been replaced by PCI Express. A motherboard will have a PCI Express x16 slot or an AGP slot, but not both.

1.2.4. Expansion cards

Expansion cards , also known as an add-on card, internal card or interface adapter, an expansion card is an electronic board or card added in a desktop computer or other non-portable computer to give that computer a new ability, such as the ability to connect to another computer using a network cable.

Below is a list of expansion cards that could be installed in an available expansion slot.

- interface card (ATA /IDE / USB)
- Modem
- Network Card
- Sound Card
- Video Card
- TV tuner card

ATA

- Short for AT Attachment
- It is an interface used to connect such devices as hard disk drives, CD-ROM drives, and other types of drives in IBM compatible computers
- more commonly known as IDE or ATA-1

Modem

- Short for MODulator/DEModulator

- The modem is a hardware device that enables a computer to send and receive information over telephone lines.

NIC

- Short for Network Interface Card
- a NIC is also commonly referred to as a network adapter
- It is an expansion card that enables a computer to connect to a network using an Ethernet cable with a RJ-45 connector.

Sound card

- Also known as a sound board or an audio card
- a sound card is an expansion card or integrated circuit that provides a computer with the ability to produce sound that can be heard by the user either over speakers and/or headphones

Video adapter

- Also known as a graphics card, video card, video board, or a video controller
- It is an internal circuit board that allows a display device such as a monitor to display a picture from the computer.

A TV tuner

- A TV tuner card can turn your computer into a television by providing a jack for you to plug up your TV cable. A capture card not only receives TV input but can capture that input into video and audio files.

1.2.5. Ports, Cables and Connectors

Port: - is a point at which a peripheral attaches to or communicated with a system unit so the peripheral can send the data to or receive information from the computer.

Cables (bus):- is an electrical channel along which bits transfer within the circuitry of a computer, allowing devices both inside and attached to the system unit to communicate.

Connectors: - are used to connect port and cables (devices).

Devices can plug into a port that comes directly off the motherboard, such as a USB, FireWire (IEEE 1394), sound, video, PS/2, network, serial, or parallel port. Or a port such as an eSATA, FireWire, USB, parallel, serial, video, or SCSI port can be provided by an expansion card. PS/2 Ports_(Mouse (green) + Keyboard): The PS/2 Ports are simple, 6-pin, low-speed serial connections commonly dedicated to a keyboard and mouse.

VGA Port (video graphics array): used to connect the monitor to the computer. Video cards and display devices might use one or more of the following video ports:

15-pin VGA port : This is the standard analog video method of passing three separate signals for red, green, and blue (RGB), which older video cards and CRT monitors use.

DVI (Digital Visual Interface): This method is the digital interface standard used by digital monitors such as a digital LCD monitor and digital TVs (HDTV). For a video card that only has a DVI port, you can purchase a VGA converter so you can connect a standard VGA video cable to use a regular analog monitor.

S-Video (Super-Video) port: An S-Video port sends two signals over the cable, one for color and the other for brightness, and is used by some high-end TVs and video equipment. It uses a 4-pin round port.

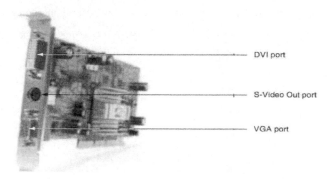

Figure 1.4: Video ports

USB PORTS

USB ports are fast becoming the most popular ports for slower I/O devices such as printers, mice, keyboards, scanners, joysticks, modems, digital cameras, fax machines, barcode readers, external floppy drives, external hard drives, and digital telephones. USB is much easier to configure and faster than regular serial or parallel ports and uses higher-quality cabling.

Fig 1.5: USB connector and its icon

Note: Even though USB devices are hot-swappable, it's not always a good idea to plug or unplug a device while it is turned on. If you do so, especially when using a low-quality USB cable, you can fry the port or the device if wires in the USB connectors touch (creating a short) as you plug or unplug the connectors. Also, to protect the data on a USB storage device, double-click the Safely Remove Hardware icon in the notification area.

Fire wire (IEEE 1394) ports

FireWire and i.Link are common names for another peripheral bus officially named IEEE 1394 (or sometimes simply called 1394). FireWire is similar in design to USB, using serial transmission of data. FireWire devices are hot-pluggable and up to 63 FireWire devices can be daisy chained together.

Serial ports

Serial ports were originally intended for input and output devices such as a mouse or an external modem. Serial ports are sometimes called DB9 and DB25 connectors. DB stands for data bus and refers to the number of pins on the connector. The DB9 port is the most common. Serial ports are almost always male ports, and parallel ports are almost always female ports. A serial port is provided by the motherboard or might be provided by an adapter card called an I/O controller card. The controller card is likely to also provide a parallel port or game port. A serial port on the motherboard can be enabled and disabled in BIOS setup.

Parallel Port (DB25 Parallel Port)

Printers and other devices are said to be either parallel or serial. Parallel means the device is capable of receiving more than one bit at a time. Most modern printers are parallel.

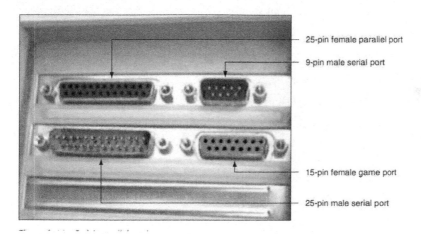

                             — 25-pin female parallel port

                             — 9-pin male serial port

                             — 15-pin female game port

                             — 25-pin male serial port

Figure 1.6: Serial, parallel, and game ports

Serials ports can go by more than one name. Because a serial port conforms to the interface standard called RS-232c (Reference Standard 232 revision c or Recommended Standard 232 revision c), it is sometimes called an RS-232 port. A serial port might also be called a COM1 (Communications port 1) or COM2 port. The controller logic on a motherboard that manages serial ports is called UART (Universal Asynchronous Receiver-Transmitter) or UART 16550, which leads us to sometimes call a serial port a UART port. By the way, the UART chip might also control an internal modem that uses resources normally assigned to the serial port.

Infrared transceivers

An infrared transceiver, also called an IrDA (Infrared Data Association) transceiver or an IR transceiver, provides an infrared port for wireless communication. Television remote controls communicate with the TV or set top box using infrared transmission. On desktop and notebook computers, infrared can be used by wireless keyboards, mice, cell phones, PDAs, and printers. On notebooks, an infrared receiver is often used for communication between the notebook and a PDA (such as a Pocket PC, Blackberry, or smart phone) to transfer information. Also, an older PC might use an infrared device to connect to a network.

Ethernet Port (RJ-45 port):- RJ (Registered jack)-45 connectors, are most commonly found on Ethernet networks that use twisted pair cabling.

Modem port (RJ-11 Port):- used to connect telephone cable from computer to Telephone Jack.

Mini Audio Jack:- used to connect computer to the speaker.

1.2.6. Storage devices

All information needs to be stored somewhere. It's a simple fact of life, at your office, you may have letters, contracts, and so on that needs to be storing somewhere to make them easily accessible and retrievable. With computers, you have various types of electronic information to store, including data files, application files, and configuration files. Storage devices in computer system are used to store files and programs. There two kinds of storage: temporary and permanent. The processor uses temporary storage, called primary storage or memory, to temporarily hold both data and instructions while it is processing them. However, when data and instructions are not being used, they must be kept in permanent storage, sometimes called secondary storage, such as a hard drive, CD, DVD, or USB drive. Primary storage is much faster to access than permanent storage.

1.2.7. Secondary Memory

Secondary storage devices are used to store data permanently. The most important difference between primary and secondary storage is that secondary storage is permanent. When you turn off your computer, the information in secondary storage remains intact. Secondary storage devices are often grouped in these three categories: hard drives, optical drives, and removable storage.

Hard Drives

- The computer stores information that is permanent, on the Hard Disk platter.
- The Hard Disk is sealed in the Hard Disk Drive.
- The disc is made from **aluminium** with coating of magnetic material such as ferric oxide or chromium oxide.
- The Hard Disk Drive is very sensitive to shock and electrostatic discharge.
- Data is stored on the surface of a platter in **sectors and tracks**
- **Tracks are concentric circles**, and **sectors are pie-shaped** wedges on a track with magnetic marking and an ID number, Sectors have a sector header and an error correction code (ECC).

Basic Hard Disk Drive Components

- Disk platters- round, flat disks designed to store information in the form of magnetic patterns.
- Read/write heads- reads/writes data

- Head actuator mechanism- moves the head across the disk
- Spindle motor (inside platter hub)- The motor that spins/rotates the platters
- Logic board (controller or Printed Circuit Board)- controls the activity of the other components and communicates with the rest of the PC.
- Cables and connectors- Interface connectors , power connectors
- Configuration items (such as jumpers or switches)

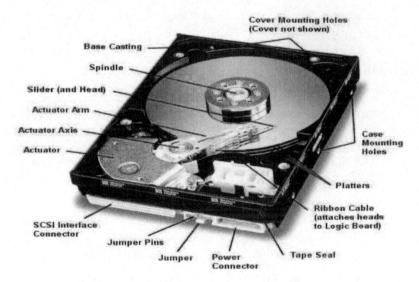

Figure 1.7: Internal Components of Hard disk

Hard disk interfaces

Hard drives have different ways to interface with the computer.

You can classify hard disk interfaces as internal and external:

Internal interfaces

1. ATA/IDE
2. SATA
3. SCSI
4. PATA/EIDE

External interfaces

1. eSATA (external SATA)
2. SCSI
3. USB
4. FireWire

ATA/IDE interfaces

ATA interfaces are used to connect hard drives and other drives such as CD, DVD, tape and Blu-ray drives with a computer system. ATA (AT Attachment) is the official name of IDE (Integrated Drive Electronics) and IDE is a marketing term.

PATA/EIDE interfaces

Parallel ATA, sometimes called the EIDE (Enhanced IDE) standard or the IDE standard, is slower than SATA and allows for only two connectors on a motherboard for two data cables. Using this interface, a motherboard can accommodate up to four IDE devices in one system.

SATA interfaces

SATA uses a serial data path rather than the traditional parallel data path. Serial ATA interfaces are much faster and newer than PATA interfaces and are used by all types of drives, including hard drives, CD, DVD, Blu-ray, and tape drives. In addition to internal SATA connectors, the motherboard or an expansion card can provide external SATA (eSATA) ports for external drives.

SCSI Technology

SCSI (pronounced "scuzzy") stands for Small Computer System Interface, and is a standard for communication between a subsystem of peripheral devices and the system bus. SCSI standards can be used by many internal and external devices, including hard drives, CD-ROM drives, DVD drives, printers, and scanners. The SCSI bus can support up to 7 or 15 devices, depending on the SCSI standard.

Hard disk Installation

1. Turn off the computer, unplug the external cables, and open computer cover. Mount the Hard Disc in the designated place in the computer.
2. Connect 40 pin interface cable and power cable. Make sure that the directions of the cables are correct and match the shape of the receptacles when connecting cables. Incorrect cable connection may damage the Hard Disk Drive.
3. Making Computer Detect the new Device. Run the CMOS (BIOS) set-up program to detect the new Hard Disk Drive.
4. Partitioning and formatting the Drive.

There are two types of formatting:

1. low- Level formatting (physical formatting)
2. High-Level formatting (logical formatting)

Low Level Formatting

- creates the tracks and sectors on a hard disk

- stays unchanged for the entire life of the drive unless the drive is re-formatted
- done at the factory on all modern drives

High Level Formatting

- The operating system writes the file system structures necessary for managing files and data on the disk.
- These data structures enable the operating system to manage the space on the disk, keep track of files, and even manage defective areas so they do not cause problems.

Partitioning

- Partitioning is creating multiple volumes/logical drives on the drive
- A volume or logical drive is any section of the disk to which the operating system assigns a drive letter or name.
- Partitioning is required because a hard disk is designed to be used with more than one operating system or file system.
- Every hard disk drive must have at **least one partition** on it and can have **up to four partitions**, each of which can support the same or different type file systems
- Windows normally uses two types of partitions, called **primary and extended.**
- There can be up to four total partitions on a drive.
  Only primary partitions can be marked **active (bootable).**

1.2.8. Optical Disk Drives

Optical disks are popular storage media for multimedia data, and they are the most popular way of distributing software. There are two most common types of optical disks:

1. CD (Compact Disc)
2. DVD (Digital Versatile Disc)

CD (Compact Disc)

CD can store 700BM of information. Data is stored only on one side of the disc.

There are three basic types of CDs:

1. CD-ROM (Compact Disc Read Only Memory) - This kind of is read only i.e. you can't write data to such CDs or you can't erase from them. Data is only accessed/read from these CDs.
2. CD-R (Compact Disc Recordable) - It is also called WORM (Write Once and Read Many). These CDs can be written on once. But then after, you can't rewrite on it or erase data from it. After you first wrote data on such discs, then only thing you can do to read data from them.
3. CD-RW (Compact Disc Read-Write) - They are also called erasable optical discs. You can write data as many times as you want on such CDs. You can also erase the content of such CDs.

If a CD drive can only read a CD and not write to it, the drive is called a CD-ROM drive. Two types of CD drives that can record or write to a CD are CD-R (CD-recordable) drives and CD-RW (CD-rewritable) drives, the latter of which allow you to overwrite old data with new data. CD-RW drives have made CD-R drives outdated.

DVD (Digital Versatile Disc)

DVD stands for Digital Versatile Disc. But some people mistakenly call it Digital Video Disc. It is a relatively new technology that is introduced recently. It is similar to CD except that it can store large amounts of data and it has narrow tracks than CD. It can store 4 -17GB of information.

How optical drive interface with the motherboard

When you purchase a CD or DVD drive, consider how the drive will interface with the system. Optical drives can interface with the motherboard in several ways:

- Using a parallel ATA interface (also called an EIDE interface); the drive can share an EIDE connection and cable with another drive. However, know that if the other drive is a hard drive, hard drive performance might suffer. Parallel ATA is the most popular interface method for CD and DVD drives, and is also used by tape drives and Zip drives.
- Using a serial ATA interface (also called a SATA interface); the drive is the only drive on the serial ATA cable. Serial ATA optical drives are not yet commonplace, but are expected to eventually be more popular than parallel ATA drives.
- Using a SCSI interface with a SCSI host adapter.
- Using a portable drive and plugging into an external port on your PC, such as a USB port, FireWire port, or SCSI port

1.2.9. Primary Storage

Primary storage is provided by devices called memory or RAM (random access memory) located on the motherboard and on some adapter cards. RAM chips are embedded on a small board that plugs into the motherboard. These small RAM boards are called memory modules, and the most common type of module is the DIMM (dual inline memory module).

Random Access Memory (RAM)

- The kind of memory used for holding programs and data being executed is called random access memory or RAM.
- Memory is the workspace for the processor.
- It is a **temporary storage** area where the programs and data being operated on by the processor must reside.
- **Volatile memory, which** means that the contents are erased when the computer is powered off.
- **More RAM** means **more capacity** to hold and process large programs and files , as well as enhance system performance
- **RAM** can be found in various Places in a computer system. For example, most new **video and sound cards** have their own built-in RAM, as do many types of printers.

Relationship between RAM, Hard disk and CPU

The relationship between RAM, Hard disk and CPU can be simply expressed using office desk and file cabinet analogy.

- **The file cabinet** represents the system's **hard disk**---where both programs and data are stored for long-term safekeeping.
- **The desk** represents the system's **main memory**, which allows **the person working at the desk** (acting as the **processor**) direct access to any files placed on it. For you to work on a particular file, it must first be retrieved from the cabinet and placed on the desk.

- If the desk is large enough, you might be able to have several files open on it at one time; likewise, if your system has more memory, you can run more or larger programs and work on more or larger documents.
- Adding hard disk space to a system is similar to putting a bigger file cabinet in the office
- One difference between this analogy and the way things really work in a computer is that when a file is loaded into memory, it is a copy of the file that is actually loaded; the original still resides on the hard disk

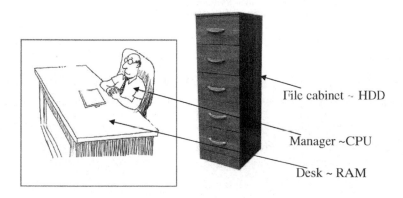

File cabinet ~ HDD

Manager ~CPU

Desk ~ RAM

Figure 1.8: Office desk analogy for storage devices

Installing a DIMM on a PC

1. Turn off the computer, unplug it, and take off the case cover.
2. Locate the memory slots.
3. Remove the old memory (if applicable).
4. Install the RAM. To do this, first locate the little notches on the pin-side of the module. These notches (usually two) will line up with keys

on the memory socket itself, to ensure proper alignment. With the ejector clips in the open position, position the module over the slot and begin pressing the module down into the slot. You will need to press down pretty hard. As you press down, the module will sink into place and the ejector clips will close themselves to lock the module into place.

5. Repeat previous step for all remaining DIMMs you wish to install.
6. Test it. Before you put your case back on, power on your system and make sure it correctly tallies the RAM.
7. Close up the case.

1.2.10. Power supply

A **power supply,** also known as a **power supply unit (PSU)**, is a box inside a computer case that supplies power to the motherboard and other installed devices. A power supply receives 110–120 volts of AC power from a wall outlet and converts it to a much lower DC voltage such as 3.3, 5, and 12 volts DC.

AC AND DC

- **Electricity** can be either **AC, alternating current, or DC, direct current.**
- **alternating current (AC)** goes back and forth, or oscillates, rather than traveling in only one direction
- **Direct current (DC)** travels in only one direction and is the type of current that most electronic devices require, including computers.
- **rectifier** is a device that converts AC to DC
- **Inverter** is a device that converts DC to AC.

- **A transformer** is a device that changes the ratio of voltage to current.
- A **capacitor** is an electronic device that can hold an electrical charge for a period of time and can smooth the uneven flow of electricity through a circuit.

Power Supply Connectors

Every PC power supply has connectors that attach to the motherboard, providing power to the motherboard, processor, memory, chipset, integrated components (such as video, LAN, USB, and FireWire), any cards plugged into bus slots and disk drives. The following are types of power supply connectors.

Molex Connector: is a four-wire connector that delivers +5-volt and +12-volt signals from the power supply. It is a power connector for hard drives and CD drives.

Mini Connector: is a two pin connector that delivers a +5 –volt signal from the power supply. A variation of this connector has four wires and delivers +12 –volt and +5 volt signal.

P1 20+4 pin connector: it is the main power connector (usually called P1). It is the connector that goes to the motherboard to provide it with power. The connector has 20 or 24 pins. One of the pins belongs to the PS-ON wire (it is usually green).

Electrical power issues

A PC's power supply is the source and cause of more component failures than any other component of the PC. A faulty power supply can burn out or weaken the electrically fragile electronics. Common power delivery problems encountered by the power supply are as follows:

Power surges: A power surge is a short duration increase in household current. Power surges may be caused internally when you switch on an appliance such as an air conditioner, or an electric dryer, demands an unusually high amount of current from the grid. The sudden jump in electricity spreads throughout the home instantaneously, briefly exposing electrical components to increased voltage. Computers and other sensitive devices that aren't plugged into surge protectors may be affected.

Spikes: Spikes are instantaneous, very high-intensity bursts of electrical power. One source of spikes is nearby lightning strikes that transmit electromagnetic energy into the home through power lines, telephone lines and other access points. Another common spike occurs at the instant electricity is restored after a blackout on the local utility grid. In these cases, voltage frequently initially spikes before resolving to a normal level.

Power sags: Sags are intermittent drops in voltage. When they last more than a short duration, they're generally known as brown-outs. A brown-out may be a planned event by an electrical utility that's reaching maximum capacity, such as during a summer heat wave. Or it may be an in-home phenomenon that results from a number of high-drain appliances simultaneously demanding more electricity than an outdated main power panel and/or wiring can deliver.

Brownout: A brownout is a voltage deficiency that occurs when the need for power exceeds power availability. Brownouts typically last for a few minutes, but can last up to several hours, as opposed to short-term fluctuations like surges or spikes.

Blackout: A blackout, or power outage, is a complete loss of utility power, whether short- or long-term. Blackouts cause reduced productivity, lost revenue, and system crashes and data loss. Unplanned outages may occur as aging electrical grids and building circuits are overwhelmed by high demand. Blackouts are particularly dangerous at sites where safety or life support rely on power, such as hospitals, treatment centers and power plants.

Protecting the Power supply

There are a number of devices you can use to protect your PC and its power supply from the problems associated with AC power.

Surge suppressors

- A device used to filter out the effects of voltage spikes and surges that are present in commercial power sources and smooth out power variations
- A good surge suppressor will protect your system from most problems
- Most power strips with surge protection have a red indicator light. If the light goes out, this means that the unit is not providing protection
- Most power strip/surge protectors should be replaced every year or so. If the light starts flashing before then, the power strip is failing and should be replaced.

Uninterruptible power supply (UPS)

- For complete protection from power fluctuations and outages, the uninterruptible power supply (UPS) is recommended
- A UPS is an inline battery backup. When properly installed between a computer and the wall outlet, a UPS device protects the computer from surges and acts as a battery when the power dips or fails
- Many models can also interact with the computer and initiate a safe shutdown in the event of a complete power failure. They do this by means of software that runs in the background and is set in action by a signal through one of the computer's COM ports when the power goes down

Line conditioners

- **Line conditioners**, also called **power conditioners**, regulate, or condition, the power, providing continuous voltage during brownouts. These voltage regulators can come as small desktop units. They provide a degree of protection against swells or spikes and raise the voltage when it drops during brownouts or sags. Power conditioners are measured by the load they support in watts, volt-amperes (VA), or kilovolt-amperes (kVA).

Protect the equipment against static electricity

Electrostatic discharge (ESD), commonly known as static electricity is an electrical charge at rest. ESD can cause two types of damage in an electronic component: catastrophic failure and upset failure. A catastrophic failure destroys the component beyond use. An upset failure damages the component so that it does not perform well, even though it may still function to some degree. Upset failures are more difficult to detect because they are not consistent and not easily observed. Both types of failures permanently affect the device.

To protect the computer against ESD, always ground yourself before touching electronic components, including the hard drive, motherboard, expansion cards, processors, and memory modules. You can ground yourself and the computer parts by using one or more of the following static control devices or methods:

- **Ground bracelet**. Also called an **antistatic wrist strap or ESD bracelet**, is a strap you wear around your wrist.

• **Antistatic gloves**. You can purchase antistatic gloves designed to prevent an ESD discharge between you and a device as you pick it up and handle it

Figure 1.9: A ground bracelet, which protects PC components from ESD.

Troubleshooting power supply

A weak or faulty power supply can create a number of problems for the peripheral devices installed inside the system unit, especially the motherboard and disk drives. Unexplained or intermittent memory or hard disk errors are commonly caused by a faulty or failing power supply. Possible symptoms of a problem with the power supply are:

- The PC appears "dead"—no lights, no spinning drive, or fan.
- The PC sometimes halts during booting. After several tries, it boots successfully.
- Error codes or beeps occur during booting, but they come and go.
- You smell burnt parts or odors. (Definitely not a good sign!)
- The PC powers down at unexpected times.

- The PC appears dead except you hear a whine coming from the power supply

- Spontaneous rebooting or intermittent lockups during normal operation

The following are simple methods to help you solve some common power supply–related problems:

- Check the AC power input. Make sure the cord is firmly seated in the wall socket and in the power supply socket. Try a different cord.

- Check the DC power connections. Make sure the motherboard and disk drive power connectors are firmly seated and making good contact. Check for loose screws.

- Check the DC power output. Use a digital multimeter to check for proper voltages. If it's below spec, replace the power supply.

- Check the installed peripherals. Remove all boards and drives and retest the system. If it works, add items back in one at a time until the system fails again. The last item added before the failure returns is likely defective.

Problems with external power

A brownout (reduced current) of the house current might cause symptoms of electrical power problems. If you suspect the house current could be low, check other devices that are using the same circuit. A copy machine, laser printer, or other heavy equipment might be drawing too much power. Remove the other devices from the same house circuit. **A line conditioner** might solve the problem of **intermittent errors** caused by noise in the power line to the PC. Try installing a line conditioner to condition voltage to the PC.

Problems that come and go

If a system boots successfully to the Windows desktop, you still might have a power system problem. Some problems are intermittent; that is, they come and go. Here are some symptoms that might indicate an intermittent problem with the electrical system after the boot:

- The computer stops or hangs for no reason. Sometimes it might even reboot itself.
- Memory errors appear intermittently.
- Data is written incorrectly to the hard drive.
- The keyboard stops working at odd times.
- The motherboard fails or is damaged.
- The power supply overheats and becomes hot to the touch.
- The power supply fan becomes very noisy or stops

Generally, intermittent problems (those that come and go) are more difficult to solve than a dead system. There can be many causes of intermittent problems, such as an inadequate power supply, overheating, and devices and components damaged by ESD.

Problems with a faulty power supply

If you suspect the power supply is faulty, you can test it using either a power supply tester (the easier method) or a multimeter (the more tedious method). However, know that a power supply that gives correct voltages when you measure it might still be the source of problems, because power problems can be intermittent. Also be aware that an ATX power supply monitors the range of voltages provided to the motherboard and halts the motherboard if voltages are inadequate. Therefore, if the power supply appears "dead," your best action is to replace it.

1.3. External Components

1.3.1. Case

- A computer case is the enclosure that encases all the components of a computer.
- All the computer's components mount to the inside of the case the case is essentially the mounting platform for all the electronic devices that make up the computer.
- Typically, cases are square or rectangular boxes, usually beige in color (although the current trend is for all-black cases and matching peripherals), and made of steel, aluminum, or plastic.

Functions of a case

1. The case or enclosure forms the mechanical foundation of every PC. Every other subassembly is bolted securely to this chassis
2. The chassis is electrically grounded through the power supply. Grounding prevents the building up or discharge of static electricity from damaging other subassemblies.

Types of computer cases

There are 3 general classifications of cases:

- Desktop case
- Tower case
- notebook cases

Desktop case

- Come in a variety of shapes and sizes

- offer a lot more upgrade potential than baby case
- Two external drive bays and two internal drive bays
- Support power supply (usually 200-250 wt)

Tower case

- Designed to hold the maximum number of drives
- Four drive bays and four internal drive bays
- Often used for servers
- Power supply (300w+)

Notebook cases

- are used for portable computers
- The cost and power of notebook systems vary widely
- Notebook designs are often highly proprietary, but are generally designed to conserve space, allow portability, use less power, and produce less heat.

Figure 1.9: Full-size tower case for an ATX motherboard

1.3.2. Monitors and displays

The primary output device of a computer is the monitor. The two necessary components for video output are the **monitor** and the **video card** (also called the video controller, video adapter, and graphics adapter) or a video port on the motherboard.

The two main categories of monitors are:

- **CRT** (cathode-ray tube) monitor-takes up a lot of desk space and costs less
- **LCD** (liquid crystal display) monitor-frees your desk space, looks cool, and costs more

The older CRT technology was first used in television sets, and the newer LCD technology was first used in notebook PCs. LCD monitors are also called **flat panel monitors** for desktop computers.

Changing monitor settings

Settings that apply to the monitor can be managed by using the monitor buttons and Windows utilities. Using the monitor buttons, you can adjust the horizontal and vertical position of the screen on the monitor surface and change the brightness and contrast settings. For laptops, the brightness and contrast settings can be changed using function keys on the laptop. Also, some CRT monitors have a degauss button. Press the degauss button to eliminate accumulated or stray magnetic fields around the monitor, which can cause a CRT monitor to flicker or have wavy lines.

To use Windows Vista to adjust resolution and refresh rate, follow these steps:

1. Right-click the Windows desktop and select Personalize from the shortcut menu or you can open the Control Panel and click Adjust screen resolution.

2. Use the sliding bar to adjust the resolution. Then click Apply. The screen changes and the message "Do you want to keep these display settings?" appears. Click Yes.

3. To change the refresh rate, click Advanced Settings. The monitor property box opens. Click the Monitor tab. Select the largest refresh rate and click Apply.

4. Click OK to close the Display Settings box.

1.3.3. Projectors

A monitor gives excellent performance when only two or three people are viewing, but you may want to use a projector in addition to a monitor when larger groups of people are watching. Projectors are great in the classroom, for sales presentations, or for watching the Super Bowl with your friends. To use a projector, you'll need an extra video port. Most notebook computers are designed to be used with projectors and provide the extra **15-pin video port** or **S-Video port**. To use a projector, plug in the projector to the extra port and then turn it on. For a notebook computer, use a function key to activate the video port. For most notebooks, you can toggle the function key to:

(1) Use the LCD display and not use the port

(2) Use both the LCD display and the port

(3) Use the port and don't use the LCD display.

Also, when you first use the projector, it will show a mirrored image of exactly what you see on your LCD panel. If you want to make the projector an extension of the desktop, you can open the Vista Display Setting box or the XP Display Properties box, select the second monitor, and select Extend the desktop onto this monitor. The projector now works as a dual monitor.

Troubleshooting monitors and video cards

For monitors as well as other devices, if you have problems, try doing the easy things first. For instance, try to make simple hardware and software adjustments. Many monitor problems are caused by poor cable connections or bad contrast/brightness adjustments.

Typical monitor and video card problems and solutions

☞ *Problem: Power light (led) does not go on; no picture*

For this problem, try the following:

- Is the monitor plugged in? Verify that the wall outlet works by plugging in a lamp, radio, or similar device. Is the monitor turned on? Look for a cutoff switch on the front and on the back. Some monitors have both.

- If the monitor power cord is plugged into a power strip or surge protector, verify that the power strip is turned on and working and that the monitor is also turned on.

- If the monitor power cord is plugged into the back of the computer, verify that the connection is tight and the computer is turned on.

- A blown fuse could be the problem. Some monitors have a fuse that is visible from the back of the monitor. It looks like a black knob that you can remove (no need to go inside the monitor cover). Remove the fuse and look for the broken wire indicating a bad fuse.

- The monitor might have a switch on the back for choosing between 110 volts and 220 volts. Check that the switch is in the right position.

- The problem might be with the video card. If you have just installed the card and the motherboard has onboard video, go into BIOS setup and disable the video port on the motherboard.

- Verify that the video cable is connected to the video port on the video card and not to a disabled onboard video port.
- If none of these solutions solves the problem, the next step is to take the monitor to a service center.

Note: A monitor retains a charge even after the power cord is unplugged. If you are trained to open a monitor case to replace a fuse, unplug the monitor and wait at least 60 minutes before opening the case so that capacitors have completely discharged.

☞ *Problem: Power led is on, no picture on power-up*

For this problem, try the following:

- Check the contrast adjustment. If there's no change, leave it at a middle setting.
- Check the brightness or backlight adjustment. If there's no change, leave it at a middle setting.
- Make sure the cable is connected securely to the computer.
- If the monitor-to-computer cable detaches from the monitor, exchange it for a cable you know is good, or check the cable for continuity.
- If this solves the problem, reattach the old cable to verify that the problem was not simply a bad connection.
- Test a monitor you know is good on the computer you suspect to be bad. If you think the monitor is bad, make sure that it also fails to work on a good computer.
- If the monitor works while the system boots up, but the screen goes blank when Windows starts to load, the problem is more likely to be with Windows than with the monitor or video card. Try booting Windows in Safe Mode, which you will learn to do later in the chapter. Safe Mode

allows the OS to select a generic display driver and low resolution. If this works, change the driver and resolution.

- Reseat the video card. For a PCI card, move the card to a different expansion slot. Clean the card's edge connectors, using a contact cleaner purchased from a computer supply store.

- If there are socketed chips on the video card, remove the card from the expansion slot and then use a screwdriver to press down firmly on each corner of each socketed chip on the card. Chips sometimes loosen because of temperature changes; this condition is called chip creep.

- Trade a good video card for the video card you suspect is bad. Test the video card you think is bad on a computer that works. Test a video card you know is good on the computer that you suspect is bad. Whenever possible, do both. Go into BIOS setup and disable the shadowing of video ROM. Test the RAM on the motherboard with diagnostic software.

- For a motherboard that is using an AGP or a PCI-Express video card, try using a PCI video card in a PCI slot. Trade the motherboard for one you know is good. Sometimes, though rarely, a peripheral chip on the motherboard can cause the problem.

- For notebook computers, is the LCD switch turned on? Function keys are sometimes used for this purpose.

- For notebook computers, try connecting a second monitor to the notebook and use the function key to toggle between the LCD panel and the second monitor. If the second monitor works, but the LCD panel does not work, the problem might be with the LCD panel hardware.

☞ *Problem: Power is on, but monitor displays the wrong characters*
For this problem, try the following:

- Wrong characters are usually not the result of a bad monitor but of a problem with the video card. Trade the video card for one you know is good.
- Exchange the motherboard. Sometimes a bad ROM or RAM chip on the motherboard displays the wrong characters on the monitor.

☞ *Problem: Monitor flickers, has wavy lines, or both*

For this problem, try the following:
- Monitor flicker can be caused by poor cable connections. Check that the cable connections are snug.
- Does the monitor have a degauss button to eliminate accumulated or stray magnetic fields? If so, press it.
- Check if something in the office is causing a high amount of electrical noise (EMI). For example, you might be able to stop a flicker by moving the office fan to a different outlet. Bad fluorescent lights or large speakers can also produce interference. Two monitors placed very close together can also cause problems.
- If the refresh rate is below 60 Hz, a screen flicker might appear. Change the refresh rate to the highest value the monitor supports.
- For older monitors that do not support a high enough refresh rate, your only cure might be to purchase a new monitor. Before making a purchase, verify that the new monitor will solve the problem

1.3.4. Keyboard and mouse

Input devices serve two distinct purposes on a PC. First, they allow the user to command and control the activities of the PC; second, input devices allow the user to capture and enter data into the PC. The input and output devices of the PC exist to allow the human operator and the PC to communicate with one another. The most common input devices are the keyboard and mouse. They are used for entering commands and data into the system.

Keyboard and mouse interfaces

There are four main interfaces for keyboards and mice:

Serial: This is the original interface used in personal computers. Although new computers no longer come with serial mice, the vast majority of computers have serial ports, so a serial mouse and keyboard is the perfect choice when the built-in PS/2 port fails.

PS/2: This is the standard mouse and keyboard interface for the vast majority of computers with ATX and similar motherboards. These computers have dedicated PS/2 mouse and keyboard ports that can be used only for PS/2 pointing devices and those adapted to PS/2. These devices *are not hot-pluggable;* plug in and remove only with the computer's power off.

Note: Many laptops have one PS/2 port. A keyboard or a pointing device can be plugged into this port. Y-connectors are available that allow both a pointing device and a keyboard to be plugged in simultaneously. However, not all Y-connectors work with all brands of laptops; there are at least two types of Y-connectors for this purpose. Make sure to match up one that will work with the brand you're using.

USB: This is the standard mouse or keyboard port for many new computers. However, because most computers still have PS/2 and keyboard mouse ports, unless the mouse or keyboard you want is available only in USB, it is a good idea to use a PS/2 mouse and keyboard. This is because there are many devices that use USB ports, but only one that can use a PS/2 mouse port, so you might as well save the USB port for some other device. Most of the feature-laden mice use USB. USB devices are recognized and installed by Windows, and many come with software disks. Windows, however, has drivers for almost all commercially available mice. USB mice are also good choices for replacements when PS/2 ports fail.

Wireless: Wireless mice and keyboard use one of the other interfaces in this list. They come in two varieties, infrared and *radio frequency* (*RF*). The RF types are usually preferred because the receiver and mouse do not have to be directly in line of site of each other. The mouse runs on battery power, so plan to have spare batteries on hand or at least hold on to a basic wired mouse in case of an emergency.

The wireless connection is made through a receiver that plugs into a USB port as shown in the figure 1.10 below. To install the device, plug the receiver into a USB port and then use the mouse.

Fig 1.10: Wireless mouse and USB receiver

Troubleshooting Keyboard

Keyboards can give problems if they are not kept clean. If dirt, food, or drink is allowed to build up, one or more keys might stick or not work properly. Chips inside the keyboard can fail, and the keyboard cable or port connector can go bad. Because of its low cost, when a keyboard doesn't work, the solution is most often to replace it. However, you can try a few simple things to repair one, as listed next:

1. If a few keys don't work, turn the keyboard upside down and bump it to dislodge debris and use compressed air to blow out debris.

2. If the keyboard does not work at all, check to see if the cable is plugged in. Maybe it's plugged into the mouse port by mistake. Next, swap it with a known good keyboard.

3. If a PS/2 keyboard does not work, try a USB keyboard. The PS/2 port might be bad. Know that some motherboards have a jumper that must be set for a PS/2 or USB keyboard. For other motherboards, the option to use a USB keyboard must be enabled in BIOS setup. And for still other motherboards, you can install a USB keyboard without changing any jumpers or BIOS settings.

Some common Keyboard problems and solutions

☞ *While working on PC, something (liquid) Spilled in to the keyboard.*

✓ *Solution*

- Remove the keyboard cable from its connection at the back of the PC. Do not wait!! You need to cut power to the device in order to avoid a possible short circuit.
- Shutdown the PC using the mouse [start>turn off computer ...].
- Tip the keyboard upside down and drain out as much of the liquid as you can.
- Try to dry the inside part of the keyboard properly by using blow dryer or direct sunlight.
- Reconnect the keyboard cable to the computer.
- Power up the computer and manipulate the keyboard to assure

47

proper functioning.

☞ *Some keys on the keyboard don't work.*

✓ *Solution*

For the quick help:

- Use On-Screen Keyboard. [Win XP/7] - to open On-Screen Keyboard: click on Start, point to Programs, point to Accessories, and point to Accessibility/ease of access, and then click On-Screen Keyboard. Then you can use the mouse to type any text.

  Or

- Turn OFF the PC and Remove the keyboard cable from its connection at the back of the PC.
- Turn the keyboard upside-down and remove the securing screws properly.
- Select the key that you want to remove. Just be careful not to damage the other key.
- Clean or adjust the site of the key properly.
- If you remove multiple keys, be sure to return them to their proper seats.
- Make sure· that the keyboard is dry while cleaning.
- Replace the cover.
- Reconnect the cable to the computer.
- Boot up the PC and check that if activated.

Mouse problems and solutions

☞ *Problem: The mouse may hang up or may not move in the correct way due to dust.*

✓ *Solution*

- Clean the mouse [mechanical mouse]:
  - Shutdown the PC.
  - Remove the mouse cable from its connection at the back of your PC.
  - Turn the mouse upside-down and remove the securing screws from the mouse case.
  - Remove the mouse ball from the cavity.
  - Clean the cavity and the mouse ball with proper available materials.
  - Look inside the mouse housing. You will see the two perpendicular bars. Use your finger nail to scrape along each bar, removing any dirt.
  - Reconnect the cable to the computer.
  - Turn ON the PC and see that if it is activated.

☞ *Problem: The new PS/2 or serial mouse doesn't work when plugged on the system running Windows XP.*

✓ **Solution**

- Restart the system.
- Plug the new mouse firmly.
- Restart the PC.
- The new mouse will be active.
- Else-use a replacement method.

1.3.5. Printer

- It is an electro-mechanical device that is used to put information from the computer onto paper.

- A printer is a device that accepts text and graphic output from a computer and transfers the information to paper, usually to standard size sheets of paper.
- Printers vary in size, speed, sophistication, and cost. In general, more expensive printers are used for higher-resolution color printing.

Printer Languages

Printer languages are commands from the computer to the printer to tell the printer how to format the document being printed. These commands manage font size, graphics, compression of data sent to the printer, color, etc

1.4. Review questions

1. What are the internal components of a computer?
2. What are the external components of a computer?
3. How do you know speed of the processor in your computer?
4. What is the difference between catch and RAM?
5. Which memory type is used to store BIOS in the system?
6. Can you damage the video card just by touching it with your hands?
7. List hardware components and their functions
8. Mention one simple PC problem you encountered at workplace and if possible suggest possible solutions for that problem.
9. What symptoms point to the need of more RAM in a PC?

Chapter Two

Disassembling and Assembling a PC

Now that we have understood and indentified the major hardware components, you get to what is arguably the most fun part of the process: disassembling and assembling your computer.

Rule of thumb: Always turn-off the power to your PC before connecting or disconnecting any device or cable!

2.1. Tools and equipment needed

You won't need many tools to assemble or disassemble your computer, in fact the only must have is the screwdriver, but if you can get most of the following together, you'll find things go a little easier.

2.1.1. Basic tools

Before you begin assembling or disassembling a computer, you will need some basic tools:

1. Phillips-head (cross-shaped) screwdriver
2. flat-head screwdriver
3. Needlenose pliers
4. Anti-static Wrist Strap
5. A large level working space
6. Paper and pen

Phillips-head   screwdriver   flat-head screwdriver

Anti-static Wrist Strap   Needlenose pliers

Figure 2.1   basic tools for assembling and disassembling a PC

2.2.   Safety precautions

Here are some important safety precautions that will help keep you and your equipment safe as you go through the process of disassembling and assembling a PC:

1. Static electricity is the biggest danger to the expensive parts you are about assemble, even a tiny shock, much too small for you to feel, can damage or ruin the delicate electronic traces, many times smaller than a human hair, that make up your CPU,RAM and other chips. It is important to use your anti-static wrist strap. Once you have the power supply installed in the case, clip the end of the wrist strap to the outside of the power supply.

Note: if you really must work on a computer and haven't got proper anti-static equipment, handle components by the edges; and regularly (once a minute or so), touch a grounded object. The **case metal** of your PC's power supply will usually be a suitable grounded object. Touch it every few minutes while you are working on your PC if you haven't got a wrist strap.

2. Turn off your computer and unplug your Power Supply before installing or removing any components—if power is flowing to components as they are installed or removed, they can be seriously damaged.

3. Make notes as you work so that you can backtrack later if necessary. (When you're first learning to take a computer apart, it's really easy to forget where everything it's when it's time to put it back together.

4. When handling motherboards and expansion cards, don't touch the chips on the boards. Hold expansion cards by the edges. Don't touch any soldered components on a card, and don't touch the edge connectors unless it's absolutely necessary. All this helps prevent damage from static electricity.

5. To protect the chip, don't touch it with a magnetized screwdriver.

6. Never ever touch the inside of a computer that is turned on

7. Be wary of sharp edges! Many lower-end PC cases have sharp, unfinished edges. Use care and take your time to avoid cutting your hands. If your case has this problem, a little time with some sandpaper before you begin construction can spare you a lot of pain.

8. Dismantling discrete electronic components such as your Power Supply or Monitor is dangerous. They contain high voltage capacitors, which can Cause a severe electric shock if you touch them. These hold a charge even

when the unit is not plugged in and are capable of delivering a fatal shock. The power supply and monitor contain enough power to kill you, even when they are unplugged.

2.3. Disassembling a PC

Disassembly Prerequisites

Things you need to do before you disassemble.

1. Shut down any running programs and turn the computer off.
2. Remove all cables (*especially the power cable*) that are attached to the computer. Remember that some cables use special screws to attach them to their ports.
3. Remove any floppy disks from their respective drives to prevent damage to either the disk or the drive.
4. After checking once more to see that all the prerequisites have been dealt with, move the computer to the work surface.
   - A PC technician needs to be comfortable with taking apart a computer and putting it back together. As you work inside a computer, be sure to use a ground bracelet, the safety precautions listed above, and the guidelines in the following list:
   1. If you are starting with a working computer, make sure important data is first backed up. Copy the data to an external storage device such as a flash drive or external hard drive.
   2. Power down the system, unplug it, and press the power button. Unplug the monitor, mouse, keyboard, and any other peripherals or cables attached and move them out of your way.
   3. To remove the cover of your PC, do the following:

- Many newer cases require you to remove the faceplate on the front of the case first. Other cases require you to remove a side panel first, and really older cases require you to first remove the entire sides and top as a single unit. Study your case for the correct approach.
- Most cases have panels on each side of the case that can be removed. It is usually necessary to only remove the one panel to expose the top of the motherboard. To know which panel to remove, look at where the ports are on the rear of the case.
- Locate the screws that hold the side panel in place. Be careful not to unscrew any screws besides these. The other screws probably are holding the power supply, fan, and other components in place
- After the screws are removed, slide the panel toward the rear, and then lift it off the case

4. Do the following to remove the expansion cards:
   - Remove any wire or cable connected to the card.
   - Remove the screw holding the card to the case
   - Grasp the card with both hands and remove it by lifting straight up. If you have trouble removing it from the expansion slot, you can very slightly rock the card from end to end (not side to side). Rocking the card from side to side might spread the slot opening and weaken the connection.
   - As you remove the card, don't put your fingers on the edge connectors or touch a chip, and don't stack the cards on top of one another. Lay each card aside on a flat surface.
5. If you plan to remove several components, draw a diagram of all cable connections to the motherboard, adapter cards, and drives. You might

need the cable connection diagram to help you reassemble. Note where each cable begins and ends, and pay particular attention to the small wires and connectors that connect the front of the case to the motherboard. It's important to be careful about diagramming these because it is so easy to connect them in the wrong position later when you reassemble.

6. Depending on the system, you might need to remove the motherboard next or remove the drives next. My choice is to first remove the motherboard. It and the processor are the most expensive and easily damaged parts in the system. To remove the motherboard do the following:

   - Document and remove all wire attachments to the motherboard.
   - Disconnect wires leading from the front of the computer case to the motherboard
   - Remove the screws that hold the motherboard to the case.
   - carefully remove it from the case

7. To remove the Power Supply do following :

   - All power connectors should be removed, including the connection to the motherboard and any auxiliary fans.
   - Remove the connection to the remote power switch at the front of the case. Orientation of the colored wires at this switch is critical. If you remove them, make sure you document well, and during re-assembly plug the computer into a fused surge protector before turning it on (this could save your motherboard and components from melting if you've reconnected improperly).

- Remove the four screws at the back of the case and gently slide the power supply out of the case.

2.4.   Assembling a PC

To reassemble a computer, reverse the process of disassembling. Do the following

1. Install components in the case in this order: power supply, drives, motherboard, and cards. When installing drives, know that for some systems, it's easier to connect data cables to the drives and then slide the drives into the bay.
2. Connect all data and power cables. Before you replace the cover, take a few minutes to double-check each connection to make sure it is correct and snug.
3. Plug in the keyboard, monitor, and mouse
4. Turn on the power and check that the PC is working properly. If the PC does not work, most likely the problem is a loose connection. Just turn off the power and go back and check each cable connection and each expansion card. You probably have not solidly seated a card in the slot. After you have double-checked, try again.

2.5. Review Questions

1. What is the first step you have to do before starting disassembling or assembling a PC?

2. List the basic tools that are needed for assembling or disassembling a computer

3. What are the important safety precautions that will help keep you safe as you go through the process of disassembling or assembling a PC?

4. What are the general procedures that a PC technician must follow while disassembling or assembling a PC?

5. List the guidelines that you must follow to remove a power supply

Chapter Three
BIOS and CMOS configuration

3.1. Defining BIOS and CMOS

BIO stands for basic input/output system, which consists of low-level software that controls the system hardware and acts as an interface between the operating system and the hardware. The BIOS is essentially the link between hardware and software in a system.

The BIOS itself is software running in memory that consists of all the various drivers that interface the hardware to the operating system. The BIOS is unique compared to normal software in that some of it is preloaded into read-only memory (or ROM), and some is loaded into RAM from disk.

The BIOS in a PC comes from three possible sources:

- Motherboard ROM
- Adapter card ROMs (such as that found on a video card)
- Loaded into RAM from disk (device drivers)

ROM chip contained a **power-on self test (POST)** program and a **bootstrap loader**. The **bootstrap program** was designed to initiate the loading of an OS by checking for and loading the boot sector from a floppy disk or, if one was not present, a hard disk. After the OS was loaded, it could call on the low-level routines (device drivers) in the BIOS to interact with the system hardware.

Tasks that the BIOS chip performs include

- Configuration and control of standard devices:
- The power-on self test (POST):

59

- The location of an operating system, to which it turns over control of the system by using the Bootstrap loader

The **CMOS (Complementary Metal-Oxide Semiconductor)** chip stores the settings that you make with the BIOS configuration program. The BIOS offers you many different options for most system components controlled by the BIOS, but until the settings are stored in the CMOS, the system is unable to run.

3.2. The BIOS and Standard Devices

The BIOS is a complex piece of firmware ("software on a chip") that provides support for the following devices and features of your system:
- Selection and configuration of storage devices, such as hard drives, floppy drives, and CD-ROM drives
- Configuration of main and cache memory
- Configuration of built-in ports, such as IDE hard disk, floppy disk, serial, parallel, PS/2 mouse, and USB
- Selection and configuration of special motherboard features, such as memory error correction, antivirus protection, and fast memory access
- Support for different CPU types, speeds, and special features
- Support for advanced operating systems, including networks, Windows 9x, and Windows 2000 (Plug and Play)
- Power management
- Storing System Settings

To enable the BIOS to perform these tasks, two other components on the motherboard work with the BIOS: the CMOS chip, also known as the RTC/NVRAM (Real-Time-Clock/Non-Volatile RAM), and the battery. The

CMOS stores the settings that you make with the BIOS configuration program and contains the system's Real-Time-Clock circuit. Power from a battery attached to the motherboard is used by the CMOS to keep its settings.

3.3. POST

The POST (power-on self test) portion of the BIOS allows the BIOS to find and report errors in the computer's hardware. For the POST to work correctly, the system must be configured correctly.

The POST checks the following parts of the computer:

- The CPU and the POST ROM portion of the BIOS
- The system timer
- Video display card
- Memory
- The keyboard
- The disk drives

The system will stop the boot process if it encounters a serious or fatal error. During the POST process, the BIOS use any one of several methods to report problems:

- Beep codes
- Onscreen error messages
- POST error codes

Beep Codes

Beep codes are used by most BIOS versions to indicate either a fatal error or a very serious error. A fatal error is an error that is so serious that the computer cannot continue the boot process. A fatal error would include a problem with the CPU, the POST ROM, the system timer, or memory. The serious error that beeps codes report is a problem with your video display card or circuit. Although systems can boot without video, seldom would you want to because you can't see what the system is doing.

Beep codes vary by the BIOS maker. Some companies, such as IBM, Acer, and Compaq, create their own BIOS chips and firmware. However, most other major brands of computers and virtually all "clones" use BIOS made by one of the "Big Three" BIOS vendors: American Megatrends (AMI), Phoenix Technologies, and Award Software (now owned by Phoenix Technologies).

As you might expect, the beep codes and philosophies used by these three companies vary a great deal. AMI, for example, uses beep codes for over 10 "fatal" errors. It also uses eight beeps to indicate a defective or missing video card. Phoenix uses beep codes for both defects and normal procedures (but has no beep code for a video problem), and the Award BIOS has only a single beep code (one long, two short), indicating a problem with video.

Note: Not all beep codes mean something bad. Nearly all BIOS programs will sound a single
Beep code to indicate that all is well and then continue the boot process.
Below are IBM BIOS Beep codes that can occur. However, because of the wide variety of models shipping with these BIOS, the beep codes may vary.

Beep	Error description	What You should try
No beeps	No power	Check the power supply connection and its functionality.
1 short beep	Normal Post computer is ok	,No need of checking , the computer is functional
Long repeating beeps	Problem with RAM	Check whether the RAM is properly seated or not and its functionality on your computer.
One long and one short beeps	Motherboard issue	Check the motherboard and its components
One long and two short beeps	Video issue	Check the video card for its functionality
Three Long Beeps	Keyboard issue	Verify that the keyboard is connected properly to the computer by turning off your computer and then disconnecting and reconnecting the keyboard to the computer.

Table 3.1: Beep codes

BIOS Boot Error Messages

Most BIOS versions do an excellent job of giving you onscreen error messages indicating what the problem is with the system. These messages can indicate problems with memory, keyboards, hard disk drives, and other components. Some systems document these messages in their manuals, or you can go to the BIOS vendors' Web site for more information. Keep in mind that the system almost always stops after the first error, so a serious problem early in the boot process will stop the system before the video card has been initialized to display error messages.

IBM BIOS Messages

With no valid MBR or bootable device found, systems with a very old IBM BIOS display the infamous ROM BASIC interpreter, which looks like this:

The IBM Personal Computer Basic
Version C1.10 Copyright IBM Corp 1981
62940 Bytes free
Ok

AMI BIOS Messages

With no valid MBR or bootable device found, systems with an AMI BIOS display the following message:

NO ROM BASIC - SYSTEM HALTED

This message is confusing to some because it seems to point to a problem with ROM BASIC, which of course is not what it really means! The AMI ROM does not include a BASIC interpreter in the ROM (neither does any other ROMs except those found in very old IBM machines), so instead of jumping into BASIC or displaying a useful message indicating there are no bootable devices, it displays this confusing message. The real meaning is the same as for all these messages, which is to say that none of the bootable devices in the boot sequence, were found to contain signature bytes indicating a valid MBR in their first physical sectors.

Award BIOS Messages

With no valid MBR or bootable device found, systems with an Award BIOS display the following message:

DISK BOOT FAILURE, INSERT SYSTEM DISK AND PRESS ENTER

So far, this appears to be the least confusing of these messages. You don't need a secret decoder ring to figure out what it is really trying to say.

Phoenix BIOS Messages

With no valid MBR or bootable device found, systems with a Phoenix BIOS display either the message

No boot device available
Strike F1 to retry boot, F2 for setup utility
Or this one:
No boot sector on fixed disk -
Strike F1 to retry boot, F2 for setup utility

Which of these two messages you see depends on whether no boot devices were found or readable, or a boot sector could be read but was found not to have the proper signature bytes.

POST error codes

POST error codes are output by the system BIOS during the Power on Self Test sequence. POST codes are typically output as hexadecimal numbers. These numbers (or codes) identify each of the various components and functions (a circuit or group of circuits) that are tested after the system is powered up.

POST card is a plug-in interface card that displays progress and error codes generated during power-on self-test (POST) of a computer. It is used to troubleshoot computers that do not start up. POST cards are inserted into an expansion slot, and are available in ISA (also supporting EISA), PCI, parallel port, and other variants (Mini PCIe, for laptop computers, is supported by some cards, but with restrictions). Information on the meaning of POST codes for different BIOSes is needed to interpret the codes. This is supplied with cards, but becomes dated as later BIOSes are issued; up-to-date information is available on manufacturers' and independent websites.

If at least the CPU, BIOS, and the I/O interface the POST card relies on are working, the system sends two-hexadecimal-digit codes to a specified I/O port (usually 80 hex) during startup, some indicating a stage in the startup procedure, others identifying errors.

3.4. Booting a Computer

The term booting comes from the phrase "lifting yourself up by your bootstraps" and refers to the computer bringing itself up to a working state without the user having to do anything but press the on button. This boot can be a "**hard boot**" or a "**soft boot**." A **hard boot**, or **cold boot**, involves turning on the power with the on/off switch. A **soft boot**, or **warm boot**, involves using the operating system to reboot. For Windows Vista, one way to **soft boot** is to click **Start**, click the right arrow, and click **Restart.** For Windows XP, one way to **soft boot** is to click **Start**, click Turn off Computer, and then click **Restart.**

3.4.1. The boot process

All PC need a process to begin their operations. Once you feed power to the PC, the tight interrelation of hardware, firmware and software enables the PC to start itself, to "pull itself up by the bootstraps "or boot itself.

The following processes are done as the power supply is switched on:

1. **The power supply performs a self-test**

   - When all voltages and current levels are acceptable (+5v, +3.0 through +6.0 is generally considered acceptable), the supply indicates that the power is stable and sends the "Power Good" signal to the motherboard.

   - The "Power Good" signal is received by the microprocessor timer chip, which controls the reset line to the microprocessor. In the absence of the "Power Good" signal, the timer chip continuously resets the microprocessor, which prevents the system from running under bad or unstable power conditions.

2. **The microprocessor timer chip receives the "Power Good" signal**

   - After the power supply is switched on, the microprocessor timer chip generates a reset signal to the processor (the same as if you held the reset button down for a while on your case) until it receives the "Power Good" signal from the power supply.

- After the reset signal turns off, the CPU begins to operate. Code in RAM cannot be executed since the RAM is empty. The CPU manufacturers pre-program the processor to always begin executing code at address "FFFF:0000" (usually the ROM BIOS) of the ROM.

3. **The CPU starts executing the ROM BIOS code**

- The CPU loads and executes the ROM BIOS code starting at ROM memory address "FFFF:0000" which is only 16 bytes from the top of ROM memory.

4. **POST (Power-On Self-Test)**

The POST is a series of diagnostic tests that run automatically when you turn your computer on. The POST tests the main components of the PC. Any errors found during the POST are reported by a combination of beeps and displayed error messages. The errors which occur during the POST can be classified as either 'fatal' or 'non-fatal'. A non-fatal error (e.g. problem in the extended memory) will typically display an error message on the screen and allow the system to continue the boot process. A fatal error (e.g. problem in the processor), on the other hand, stops the process of booting the computer and is generally signaled by a series of beep-codes. However, successful completion of the POST is indicated by a single beep.

5. **The BIOS locates and reads the configuration information stored in CMOS**

CMOS (Complementary Metal-Oxide Semiconductor) is a small area of memory (64 bytes) which is maintained by the current of a small battery attached to the motherboard. Most importantly, for the ROM BIOS startup routines (boot sequence), CMOS determines the order in which drives should be examined for an operating system (floppy disk first, CD-Rom first, or fixed disk first). Furthermore, it holds some essential information such as hard drive size, memory address location, and Date & Time.

6. **Loading the OS (Operating System)**

The BIOS will attempt booting using the boot sequence determined by the CMOS settings, and examine the MBR (Master Boot Record) of the bootable   disk.
The MBR is the information in the first sector (512 bytes) of any hard disk or diskette that identifies how and where an operating system is located so that it can be loaded into the RAM (booted).

3.4.2. Accessing the BIOS setup program

You can access or enter to the BIOS setup program by pressing a key or combination of keys during the boot process. The exact way to enter setup varies from one motherboard manufacturer to another. Table 3.2 lists the keystrokes needed to access BIOS setup for some common BIOS types.

BIOS	Keys to press during POST to access setup
AMI	Del
Award BIOS	Del
Older phoenix BIOS	Ctrl+Alt+Esc or Ctrl+Alt +s
Newer phoenix BIOS	F2 or f1
Dell computers using phoenix BIOS	Ctrl+Alt+enter

Table 3.2 Accessing the BIOS setup

For the exact method you need to use to enter setup, see the documentation for your motherboard. A message such as the following usually appears on the screen near the beginning of the boot:

Press DEL to change Setup Or Press F2 for Setup

When you press the appropriate key or keys, a setup screen appears with menus and help features that are often very user-friendly. Figure 3.3 shows a main menu for setup. On this menu, you can change the system date and time, the keyboard language, and other system features. The power menu in BIOS setup allows you to configure automatic power-saving features for your system, such as suspend mode or a sleep state.

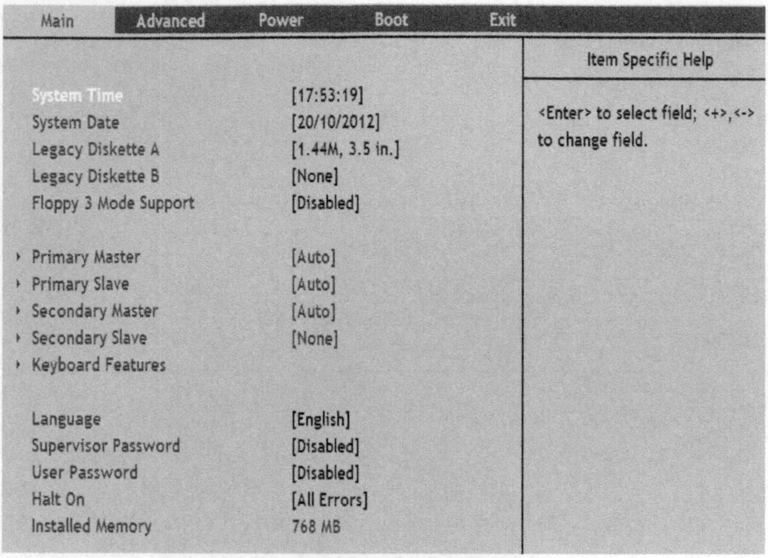

Main	Advanced	Power	Boot	Exit	

		Item Specific Help
System Time	[17:53:19]	<Enter> to select field; <+>,<->
System Date	[20/10/2012]	to change field.
Legacy Diskette A	[1.44M, 3.5 in.]	
Legacy Diskette B	[None]	
Floppy 3 Mode Support	[Disabled]	
▸ Primary Master	[Auto]	
▸ Primary Slave	[Auto]	
▸ Secondary Master	[Auto]	
▸ Secondary Slave	[None]	
▸ Keyboard Features		
Language	[English]	
Supervisor Password	[Disabled]	
User Password	[Disabled]	
Halt On	[All Errors]	
Installed Memory	768 MB	

Figure 3.3 Phoenix BIOS Setup Main menus

3.4.3. BIOS Setup Menus

Most modern BIOSs offer a menu bar at the top of the screen when you're in
the BIOS Setup that controls navigation through the various primary menus.
A typical menu bar offers the choices shown in Table 3.4

71

Set up menu	Description
Maintenance	Clears passwords and displays processor information. The maintenance menu is displayed only when the BIOS Configuration jumper is set to configure mode
Main	Processor and time/date configuration.
Advanced	Configures advanced chipset and hardware features.
Security	Sets passwords and security features.
Power	Configures power management features and power supply controls
Boot	Selects boot options.
Exit	Saves or discards changes to Setup program options

Table 3.4 BIOS set up menu

Changing the boot sequence

A figure 3.5 shows an example of a boot menu in BIOS setup. Here, you can set the order in which the system tries to boot from certain devices (called the boot sequence). Most likely when you first install a hard drive or an operating system, you will want to have the BIOS attempt to first boot from a CD and, if no CD is present, turn to the hard drive. After the operating system is installed, to prevent accidental boots from a CD or other media, change BIOS setup to boot first from the hard drive.

72

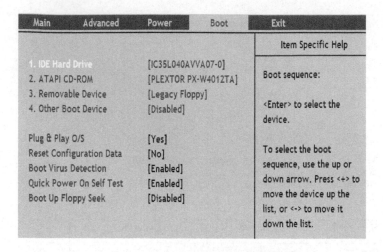

Figure 3.5 Phoenix BIOS Setup Boot menu

Exiting the BIOS setup menus

When you finish , an exit screen such as the one shown in figure 3.6 gives you various options, such as saving or discarding changes and then exiting the program, restoring default settings, or saving changes and remaining in the program.

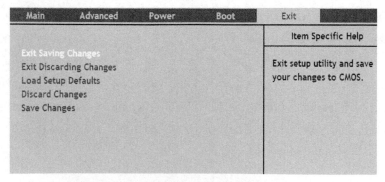

Figure 3.6 Phoenix BIOS Setup exit menu

73

Password protection to BIOS setup and to the system

Access to a computer can be controlled using a startup password, sometimes called a **user password or power-on password**. If the password has been enabled and set in BIOS setup, the startup BIOS asks for the password during the boot just before the BIOS begins searching for an OS. If the password is entered incorrectly, the boot process terminates. The password is stored in CMOS RAM and is changed by accessing the setup screen.

Note:-BIOS password is not the same as the Operating System password. Many computers provide jumpers near the chip holding CMOS RAM.

How to clear forgotten BIOS password

If you have mistakenly forgotten or lost your BIOS password or you receive a password at boot that you do not know, you will need to clear the BIOS password by one of the following methods.

- On the computer motherboard locate the BIOS clear / password jumper or dipswitch and change its position. Once this jumper has been changed, turn on the computer and the password should be cleared. Once cleared, turn the computer off and return the jumper or dipswitch to its original position.

- Additionally, when looking for the jumper / dipswitch the label of that switch can be anything; however, in most cases will be labeled **CLEAR - CLEAR   CMOS - CLR - CLRPWD - PASSWD - PASSWORD - PWD.**

- On the computer motherboard locate and remove the CMOS battery for at least 10 minutes allowing the computer to lose its information.

- If one of the above solutions do not clear the password or you are unable to locate the jumpers or solder beads, it is recommended you

contact the computer manufacturer or motherboard manufacturer for
the steps on clearing the computer password.

3.5. Review Questions

1. What is BIOS?

2. What is the difference between BIOS and CMOS?

3. Which component of a computer contains BIOS?

4. What is the function of POST?

5. How BIOS report computer problems to users?

6. How do you access or enter to the BIOS setup program in your
computer?

7. If you have computers with a Phoenix BIOS and an AMI BIOS,
will they have the same beep codes? Why or why not?

Chapter Four

Software Troubleshooting

In this section you will learn the different operating systems, how they are designed and work how to install and maintain the different operating systems. If you are a beginner it is better to start from the definition of software to make you clear about operating systems.

4.1. Computer Software

Computer hardware is directed by a set of instructions. Without these instructions, computers can do nothing. These set of instructions are called *software* (also called programs).

Software is categorized into two:

- ✓ System Software
- ✓ Application Software

4.1.1. Application Software

Application software performs useful work for the user.

These useful works could be:

- ✓ Word processing-document creation
- ✓ Spreadsheet-electronic calculation
- ✓ Communicating-email sending and reading
- ✓ Data management software's

Users use this software to perform different activities like calculation, video editing, word processing, presentation, etc. Some of the uses of application software:

Word Processing

This is the most widely used computer application. Word processing is the use of computer to produce documents that consist primarily of text. Such documents can also contain pictures, drawing, photograph, etc.

This software's are mainly used for:

- Writing letter
- Writing memos
- Producing reports

Some of the software used for word processing includes:

- Microsoft word
- WordStar
- WordPad

Spreadsheet Software

Spreadsheet software is used to organize, manipulate, and graph numeric information. It enables us to do financial analysis, and other complicated mathematical calculation electronically; such as interest rate, payroll, etc. Most common software used for this purpose include: Microsoft Excel.

Database Management system (DBMS)

Database is a collection of related data that is stored in computer. DBMS organizes the collection of data so that information can be retrieved easily. Database software allows you to create a database and to retrieve, manipulate, and update the data. Database may contain one or more tables.

Common software's that are used for DBMS:

- ✓ Microsoft Access
- ✓ Oracle
- ✓ MySQL and Microsoft SQL Server

4.1.2. Operating System

An operating system (OS) is software that controls a computer. It manages hardware, runs applications, provides an interface for users, and stores, retrieves, and manipulates files. In general, you can think of an operating system as the middleman between applications and hardware, between the user and hardware, and between the user and applications. Figure 4.1 Users and applications depend on the OS to relate to all applications and hardware components.

Several applications might be installed on a computer to meet various user needs, but a computer really needs only one operating system.

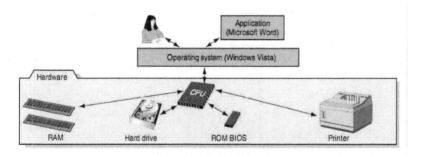

Figure 4.1 Operating System Interactions

4.2. Types of operating systems

There are different kinds of operating system available today. The following are the most commonly used operating systems.

- ❖ Disk operating systems (DOS)
- ❖ Windows XP
- ❖ Windows Vista
- ❖ Windows 7
- ❖ Window 8
- ❖ Mac OS
- ❖ Linux

Disk operating systems (dos)

In 1986, MS-DOS (also known as DOS) was introduced and quickly became the most popular OS among IBM computers and IBM-compatible computers using the Intel 8086 processors.

Windows XP

Windows XP is an upgrade of Windows 2000 and attempts to integrate Windows 9x/Me and 2000, while providing added support for multimedia and networking technologies. The two main versions are Windows XP Home Edition and Windows XP Professional, though other less significant editions include Windows XP Media Center Edition, Windows XP Tablet PC Edition, and Windows XP Professional x64 Edition.

Windows vista

Windows Vista, an upgrade to Windows XP, is the latest Windows desktop operating system by Microsoft. Vista has a new 3D user interface called the Aero user interface, which is not available for all versions of Vista and requires 1 GB of RAM and a video card or on-board video that supports the DirectX 9 graphics standard and has at least 128 MB of graphics memory.

Windows 7

With many frustrations over Windows Vista still not resolved, some consumers have dubbed Windows 7 "the ultimate Vista fix." Windows 7 is the next generation of Microsoft operating systems. Now that technicians have taken a first look at Windows 7 and have compared it to Vista, it appears that Windows 7 will perform better, be more compatible with legacy hardware and software, and provide a leaner and simpler user interface. Windows7 users have a choice of either 32-bit or 64-bit.

Window 7 editions

Microsoft offers six editions of the Windows 7 operating system. This allows an administrator to custom-fit a user's hardware and job function to the appropriate edition: Most common used editions are windows7 Professional and Windows7 Ultimate.

32-Bit vs. 64-Bit

When you hear the terms 32-bit and 64-bit, this is referring to the CPU or processor. The number represents how the data is processed. The CPU partly determines which operating system can be installed. One major consideration is the number of bits a CPU processes at a time. All desktop and laptop processors sold today from either Intel or AMD can process 64 bits at a time, but older processors handled only 32 bits. To know which type of operating system to install, you need to be aware of three categories of processors currently used on desktop and laptop computers.

1. 32-bit processors. These are known as x86 processors because Intel used the number 86 in the model number of these earlier processors. These processors must use a 32-bit operating system.

2. 64-bit processors. Intel makes several 64-bit processors for workstations or servers that use fully implemented 64-bit processing, including the Itanium and Xeon processors.

3. Processors that use underlying 32-bit processing with 64-bit instructions. These hybrid processors are known as x86-64bit processors. AMD was the first to produce one (the Athlon 64) and called the technology AMD64. Intel followed with a version of its Pentium 4 processors and called the technology Extended Memory 64

Technology (EM64T). Because of their hybrid nature, these processors can handle a 32-bit OS or a 64-bit OS. All desktop or laptop processors made after 2007 are of this type.

Windows 2000 is a 32-bit OS. Windows XP Professional x64 Edition is a 64-bit OS, hand all other Windows XP editions are 32-bit operating systems. Vista comes in either 32-bit or 64-bit versions.

Note:

- ➢ The term x86 refers to 32-bit processors and to 32-bit operating systems.
- ➢ The term x64 refers to 64-bit operating systems. For example, Microsoft offers two versions of Vista Home Premium: the x 86 versions and the x64 version.
- ➢ The term x86-64 refers to a 64-bit OS or to 32-bit processors that process 64-bit instructions such as the Intel Core2 Duo or 64-bit AMD processors (AMD64 refers specifically to these AMD processors).

Window 8

Windows 8 is a completely redesigned operating system developed from the ground up with touch screen use in mind as well as near instant - on capabilities that enable a Windows 8 PC to load and start up in a matter of seconds rather than in minutes. Windows 8 comes with a new user interface called the Windows Start Screen that is the first thing you see when you login to Windows 8. This is the main interface that Windows 8 user's use to launch applications, search for files, and browse the web. This Start screen contains tiles that represent different programs that you can launch by clicking on the title. One of the features of this new interface is that the tiles themselves are able to show you real-time information directly on the Start screen. This will allow you to use the Start screen not only as a way to start an application, but also as a way to quickly see data such as the weather, e-mail information, new RSS feed articles, etc.

Mac OS

Mac OS was named by the company Apple as "Mac System Software" in the beginning, a specially designed operating system only for 68K first Motorola processors. With own Macintosh hardware, Mac OS takes up a special role in the world of desktop systems.Currently, the Mac OS, which has its roots in the UNIX OS, is available only on Macintosh computers from the Apple Corporation.

Linux

Linux is a variation of UNIX that was created by Linus Torvalds when he was a student at the University of Helsinki in Finland. Versions of this OS are available for free, and all the underlying programming instructions (called source code) are also freely distributed. Like UNIX, Linux is distributed by several different companies; whose versions of Linux are sometimes called distributions. Popular distributions of Linux include SuSE (www.novell.com/linux/suse), RedHat (www.redhat.com), TurboLinux (www.turbolinux.com), Slackware Linux (www.slackware.com), and Ubuntu (www.ubuntu.com).

4.3. Functions of Operating system

Although there are important differences among them, all operating systems share the following four main functions:

☞ **Provide a user interface**

- Performing housekeeping procedures requested by the user, often concerning secondary storage devices, such as reorganizing a hard drive, deleting files, copying files, and changing the system date
- Providing a way for the user to manage the desktop, hardware, applications, and data

☞ **Manage files**

- Managing files on hard drives, DVD drives, CD drives, floppy drives, and other drives
- Creating, storing, retrieving, deleting, and moving files

☞ **Manage hardware**

- Managing the BIOS
- Managing memory
- Diagnosing problems with software and hardware
- Interfacing between hardware and software

☞ **Manage applications**

- Installing and uninstalling applications
- Running applications and managing the interface to the hardware on behalf of an application

4.4. Windows installation

An operating system can be installed, reinstalled, or upgraded.

4.4.1. Types of windows installation methods

❖ **Clean installation /Formatting** - A clean installation of Windows is typically performed on a new (empty) hard disk. However, it can also be performed on a system that contains an existing operating system. In such cases, unpartitioned disk space (or an existing partition that can be reused) is the target.

- ❖ **Repair installation**- A repair installation (also known as an in-place upgrade) is used to fix a damaged Windows installation. A repair installation preserves your existing Windows configuration while replacing corrupt files and repairing incorrect settings. Both Windows XP and Windows 7 support repair installations, but the methods used are different.

- ❖ **Upgrade installation** -installation of new operating system into the same folder as the old operating system, or simply saying, the new installs on top of the old. The new OS replaces the old OS but without removing all the saved data and the previous settings (such as font style, desktop colors and background) ,hardware and applications

- ❖ **Multiboot-** A multiple-boot installation is one in which multiple operating systems are installed on a computer, and the user can select which operating system to use during system startup. If you install Windows XP as an additional operating system on a computer, you still have to reinstall any applications you want to use when running Windows XP. The advantage of using a multiple-boot installation over an upgrade or clean installation is that you can retain the previous operating system and installed applications. This is useful if you want to test or experiment with Windows XP, or if you have important applications that you know will not run on Windows XP.

- ❖ **Image installation/Disk Cloning-** a complete copy of a hard disk volume on which an operating system and, usually, all required application software has been preinstalled. Images can be on a CD-media, in which case the tech runs special software (such as Norton Ghost) on the computer that copies the image on to the local hard drive.

4.4.2. Pre-installation Considerations

Before installing an operating system, you must check whether the computer meets the   following requirements for the installation:-

1. hardware requirement
2. Hardware and software compatibility
3. Type of installation to perform
4. Back up the exiting data
5. Plan for post-installation tasks

Hardware requirements

Before you can insert the Windows CD or DVD and install the operating system, you first must make sure that the machine's hardware can handle that operating system. There are different hardware requirements for different operating systems. Let us see the hardware requirements for window XP and window 7.

Minimum hardware requirements for windows XP professional

- Pentium (or compatible) 233MHz or higher processor
- 64 megabytes (MB) of RAM
- 2gigabyte (GB) hard disk with 650MB of free disk space
- A CD-ROM drive
- Video graphics adapter (VGA) or higher display adapter
- Keyboard, mouse, or other pointing device

Recommended hardware requirements for Windows XP professional

- 1.5GB of free disk space

- 128MB (4GB maximum) of RAM
- CD-ROM or DVD-ROM drive (12x or faster)
- Pentium II (or compatible) 300MHz or higher processor
- Super VGA (SVGA) display adapter and Plug and Play monitor
- Network adapter (required for network installation)
- Keyboard, mouse, or other pointing device

Basic hardware requirements to install Window 7

- 1 GHz 32-bit or 64-bit processor
- 1 GB of system memory (RAM)
- 16GB of hard disk
- A video card that supports DirectX 9 graphics with 128MB of memory
- DVD-R/W drive
- Compatible network interface card

Hardware and software compatibility

Checking hardware and software compatibility is important when you want to perform an upgrade installation of windows. You have two basic sources for this information: Microsoft and the manufacturer of the device or software. You can check whether your hardware device is compatible to the operating system or not from the Microsoft Hardware Compatibility List (HCL) through this website: http://winqual.microsoft.com/hcl/Default.aspx.

Type of installation to perform

If you are installing Windows on a new hard drive, then you are doing a clean install. If window is already installed on the hard drive and you want to install a different windows operating system, then you have three choices: clean install, upgrade or dual boot. Choose one of these.

Back up the exiting data

Whether you are installing or upgrading windows, you should backup the existing user data before installing or upgrading because the important data in the hard drive may be damaged. Before deciding to install operating system, you have to know whether the user has critical data in his computer or not.

Plan for post-installation tasks

Even though you have installed your operating system, you are not quite finished. There are a few items you must do in order to truly finish. These items include the following:

- Installing the required software's
- Installing /updating drivers
- Verify installation

Installing the required software's

After you have installed your operating system, you will want to use the computer. To use your computer, you have installed the required applications. The softwares to be installed includes such as Microsoft office, antivirus software, adobe reader and so on.

Installing /updating drivers

After you have gotten an operating system up and running, you may find that a few items aren't working properly. The drivers for some hardware devices are not found on the windows installation CD or the drivers on the installation CD are out dated. Therefore, it is a good idea to install or update the drivers for your hardware device. The Most common hardware devices that need driver software (for example, after installing windows XP) are network card, printer, sound card and scanners.

Verify installation

The last thing you should after installing any operating system is to perform verification. Verification is simply done by rebooting the computer again and log in as a user. Make sure all of the appropriate programs are there and all of the devices (such as the network card and video card) are working properly.

4.4.3. Installing the operating system

Clean Install of Windows XP

1. Power on your computer and insert bootable Windows XP Professional Setup CD-ROM into the CD drive. If your computer is not capable of booting from the CD drive, you need to enter into BIOS setup to set the CD-ROM drive as first boot device.

2. When prompted onscreen, press any key (or the specific key required) to boot the computer from the CD-ROM. Windows XP installation set up starts as figure 4.2.

Figure 4.2 Windows XP starts

3. Next You are presented with 3 options. For the purpose of this guide, press **Enter.**

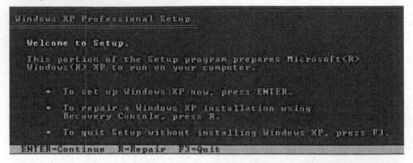

Figure 4.3 Set up window starts

Before you can install the operating system you must press **F8 and agree** to the license agreement.

4. From the screen shown in Figure 4.4, you can create and delete partitions on your hard drives. If a partition does not already exist, you must create one. To do this, highlight the unpartitioned Space" and press "C", for Create.

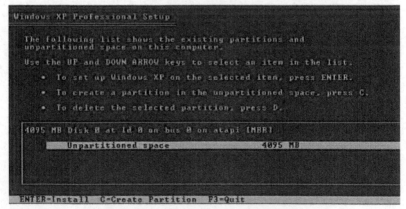

Figure 4.4 creating and deleting partitions

5. Enter the capacity you want for the new partition and press Enter. If you want to use the entire space of the drive, press Enter without making any changes.

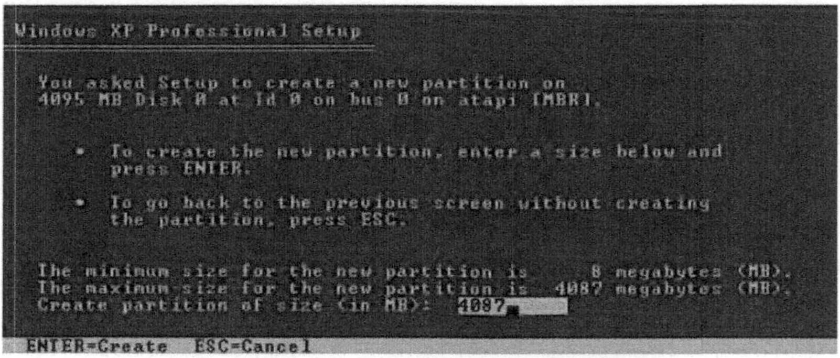

Figure 4.5 Entering capacity of a partition

6. You will be given format options for the partition: NTFS, NTFS (Quick), FAT, and FAT (Quick). Only Windows XP gives the Quick format options. If the partition is larger than 32GB's, you must choose NTFS.

WARNING: Formatting will delete all data from the drive

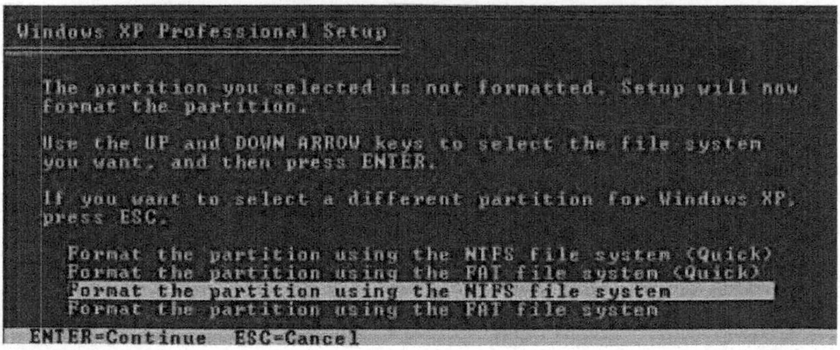

Figure 4.6 formatting a partition

The installation will now begin formatting the drive to your specifications. Depending on the size of the partition, this could take anywhere from 2 minutes to over an hour to format.

7. Select your geographical location from the list provided. Windows XP will use it to decide how to display dates, times, numbers, and currency.

8. Enter your name, the name of your organization, and your product key.

9. Enter the computer name and the password for the local Administrator account. If you are joining a domain, the computer name is the name assigned to this computer by the network administrator managing the domain controller.

10. Select the date, time, and time zone. The PC might reboot.

11. If you are connected to a network, you will be asked to choose how to configure your network settings.

12. Enter a workgroup or domain name. If you are joining a domain, the network administrator

13. Enter a workgroup or domain name. If you are joining a domain, the network administrator will have given you specific directions on how to configure user accounts on the domain.

Note: - During a normal Windows XP installation, setup causes the system to reboot three times.

Performing a clean install or dual boot

To perform a clean install of Windows Vista or a dual boot with another OS, do the following:

1. Boot directly from the Windows Vista CD or DVD. If you have trouble booting from the disc, go into BIOS setup and verify that your first boot device is the optical drive. Select your language preference, and then the opening menu shown in figure 4.8 appears. Click Install now.

2. On the next screens, enter the product key and accept the license agreement.
3. On the next screen, select the type of installation you want. Choose Custom (advanced).
4. On the next screen, you will be shown a list of partitions on which to install the OS.

Clean Install of Windows 7

Perform the following steps to perform a clean install of Windows 7:
1. Insert the Windows 7 DVD in to the machine and start the computer
2. If you are asked to Hit Any Key to start the DVD, press Enter
3. The first screen asks you to enter your language, local time, and keyboard. After filling in these fields, click next.

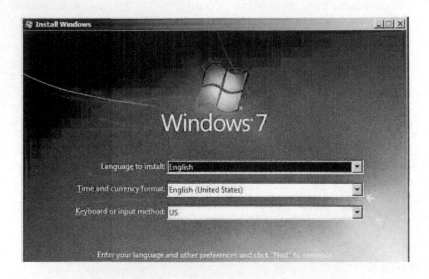

Figure 4.7 window 7 set up: setting language and time

4. At the next screen, click the Install Now button as shown in figure 4.8

5. A message shows you that Setup is starting. Read the License agreement and then check the' I accept the license term'' check box. Click Next.

6. Click Custom (Advanced) installation type

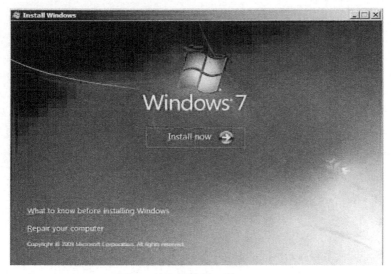

Figure 4.8 Window 7 setup screen

7. The next screen asks you where you want to install windows 7. Choose an unformatted free space or a partition (the partition will be erased) with at least 20 GB available. You can also click the Drive Options (Advanced) link to create your own partition. After you choose your partition, click next.

8. After your partition is set, the installation starts. You see the progress of the installation during the entire process. After the installation is complete, the machine reboots.

9. After the installation is complete, the user name and computer name screen appears. Type in your user name and computer name and click Next

10. Next set your password and password hint. Enter your password twice and enter your hint. click next

11. Configure your time, time zone and date. Click Next and then set your computer's current location.

12. Windows will finalize your setup and the installation will be complete.

Clean Installation of Window 8

Windows 8 Professional DVD is bootable. In order to boot from the DVD you need to set the boot sequence. Look for the boot sequence under your BIOS setup and make sure that the first boot device is set to CD-ROM/DVD-ROM. Perform the following steps to perform a clean install of Windows 8.

1. Windows 8 Bootable DVD/USB Device Insert and restart your PC. Looking **"Press any key to boot from CD or DVD."** and then hit the any key on your keyboard.

2. Windows 8 will start to boot up and Windows 8 will start loading files from the DVD/USB Device. You select your time, language; currency format and keyboard then click Next

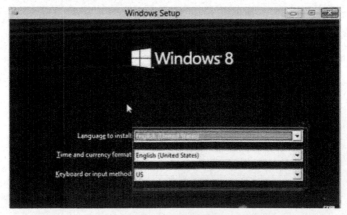

Figure 4.9 Window 8 setup : Setting language and time

3. Starting Windows 8 OS installation click on "Install Now"

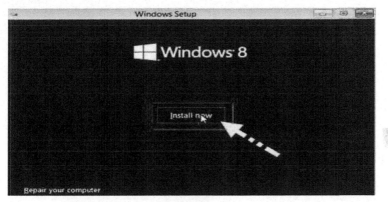

Figure 4.10 Window 8 setup install now screen

4. You can now type Windows 8 product key in the text box and click " Next ".

5. Read Windows 8 License Terms then click the check box, "I accept the licence terms" and click "Next.

6. You can select only Custom (advanced) option which basically installs a clean copy of Windows.

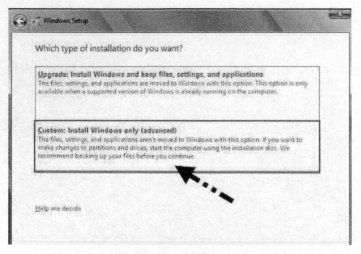

Figure 4.11 Window 8 setup : Selecting installtion type

7. Ctreat the partions based on your need

8. Windows 8 start copying all the necessary files to your hard drive through the installation process.

9. Please type your pc name in the text box then click " Next ".

10. Choose " Customize " option.

11. Then click " Sign in without a Microsoft account ".

12. Then click " Local account " option.

13. Type " User name ", you can type the password for creating password protected user account.

14. Windows 8 installation successfully completed. Finally the setup process is finished and you are presented with a completely new and unfamiliar Metro user interface. You have your most common

application right in front of you. Clicking on any tiles will launch that application

Figure 4.12 Window 8 user interface

4.5. Managing Users

After finishing installation of windows you can create accounts, passwords for accounts, install new software, and so on.

Create a user account

With user accounts, several people can easily share a single computer. Each person can have a separate user account with unique settings and preferences, such as a desktop background or screen saver.

98

To create a user account on windows XP:

1. Click on Start → control panel →users→create a new account

2. Type the name you want to give the user account, click an account type, and then click Create Account.

To create a user account on windows 7:

3. Click on start →control panel→user account

4. Click Create a new account.

5. Type the name you want to give the user account, click an account type, and then click Create Account.

User accounts types

User accounts can be customized to some extent, but basically fall into one of three categories, which are, in increasing order of privilege.

- **Guest**
- **Limited Users**
- **Administrators**

Guest Accounts

- Guest accounts have minimal access rights;
- They **can run programs but generally cannot make any changes to the system**, or save any files in shared folders.

Limited account

- Limited Users can log on, save files, and run most programs,
- but **cannot install software**, **configure Windows, change security settings**, or do much else that doesn't involve the user's own personal data

Administrator

- With a Computer Administrator account you can make any change, read or write any file, or, well, do anything that a Windows user can do.

4.6. Troubleshooting windows problems

Troubleshooting is the process of identifying a computer problem so that it can be fixed. Troubleshooting is a combination of skill and art. Troubleshooting is a skill, in that it can be learned as a process. It is an art, in that it also requires intuition, imagination. You may face different Windows problems and solutions.

You may split windows problems into the following categories:

- Problems encountered during Windows installation
- Problems encountered during Windows startup
- Problems encountered while Windows is running

4.6.1. Windows Installation Troubleshooting

If you encounter a problem while trying to install Windows XP or Windows Vista, there are a few specific things you should look at to try to fix the problem and perform a successful installation.

☞ **Problem: Legacy/Unsupported Hardware Devices**

Due to incompatible hardware windows set up may fail i.e. If windows OS that you are installing does not support the existing hardware, the windows installation may not continue. Legacy/unsupported hardware can cause Windows Setup to fail, resulting in a STOP error screen, a frozen computer, or a computer that continually reboots at the same point during the installation process.

100

✓ **Solution**

Before beginning an installation of Windows

- check Microsoft's Windows Hardware Compatibility List (http://www.microsoft.com/whdc/hcl/default.mspx)
- remove nonessential hardware from your system

☞ **Problem: Can't read read .cab, .dll**

✓ **Solution**

- Bad CD- or DVD-media discs, optical drives, or hard drives may cause **lockups**. Check the CD or DVD for scratches or dirt, and clean it up or replace it. Try a known good disc in the drive. If you get the same error, you may need to replace the drive.

☞ **Problem: Setup does not recognize hard drive during installation**

✓ **Solution**

- If possible, boot into the install disc and run the installation from there, as opposed to running setup.exe from within Windows.
- Make sure that the **HDD is detected in BIOS**.
- Try changing the SATA setting in the BIOS to AHCI, or IDE if AHCI is already set.

Other Common Windows Installation Issues

Faulty RAM modules

A malfunctioning RAM module will create havoc with Windows Setup. RAM chips can malfunction because they are defective, or if you have over clocked your PC's processor in the system BIOS, causing it to run faster than its design specifications. There are third-party memory diagnostic programs available that will run from a bootable floppy or CD that you can use to test the integrity of the system's RAM. Microsoft has a free program called the

Windows Memory Diagnostic, which you can download at http://oca.microsoft.com/en/windiag.asp.

Defective hard drive

If the system hard drive has errors on it, it's possible that Windows Setup will be unable to copy critical operating system files to it in order to complete the installation. Again, there are a number of utilities you can use to test a hard drive's integrity; the website of the manufacturer of the drive is a good starting point to look for such a utility.

Overheating system

One common environmental issue that will cause a system to either freeze up or to reboot repeatedly is if the inside of the system is not being adequately cooled. This is of particular concern if you have overclocked any of your system's components (the CPU and GPU in particular). An overheated processor, RAM module, or hard drive can all lead to a locked up system or one that spontaneously reboots. Ensure that all case fans and the CPU cooling fan are installed correctly and are operational.

Defective installation media

Installation problems can be caused by something as simple as a damaged or otherwise defective Windows installation CD or DVD. Check the surface of the CD or DVD for scratches and other marks. You can clean and polish the surface with products such as Digital Innovations' SkipDr and others.

Improper power supply load

If your system hardware requires more power than the power supply is rated to provide, it can cause instability both during and after the installation process. The best short-term solution is to remove any unnecessary hardware from your PC, thus easing the load on the power supply. From there it's time to get yourself a more powerful, high-quality power supply unit, like those available from PC Power and Cooling.

Windows Startup Troubleshooting

To determine where the boot process (start up) failure occurred, we'll focus on the following three startup stages of the boot:

Stage 1: Before the windows progress bar.

When you see the Microsoft progress bar appear, you know the Windows kernel, including all critical services and drivers, has loaded. Any problems that occur before the progress bar appears are most likely related to corrupt or missing system files or hardware. Your best Vista tools to use for these problems are Startup Repair and System Restore.

Stage 2: After the windows progress bar and before logon.

After the progress bar appears, user mode services and drivers are loaded and then the logon screen appears. Problems with these components can best be solved using Startup Repair, the Last Known Good Configuration, System Restore, and Safe Mode.

Stage 3: After logon.

After the logon screen appears, problems can be caused by startup scripts, applications set to launch at startup, and desktop settings. Use MSconfig to temporarily disable startup programs. Other useful tools to solve the problem are Software Explorer and Safe Mode.

☞ **Problems at stage 1: before the windows progress bar appears**
  ✓ **Diagnosis and Solution**

If the progress bar has not yet appeared, some portions of the windows kernel and critical drivers and services to be started by the kernel have not yet started. Therefore, the problem is with **hardware or these startup files.** Hardware that might be failing includes the power supply, motherboard, CPU, memory, hard drive, video, or keyboard. If any one of these devices is not working, the error is communicated using **beep codes, or using on-screen or voice error messages**—and then the computer halts.

Start diagnosis

- *Is the screen blank?*

If you see absolutely nothing on the screen, check that the system is getting power and the monitor is plugged in and turned on. Can you hear the spinning fan or hard drive inside the computer case? Are lights on the front of the case lit? If not, suspect that power is not getting to the system.

If you can hear a spinning drive and see lights on the front of the computer case and know the monitor works, the video card might be bad or not seated properly in its slot, the memory might be bad, the video cable might be bad, or a component on the motherboard might have failed.

- *Can startup BIOS access the hard drive?*

Error messages generated by startup BIOS that pertain to the hard drive can be caused by a variety of things.

Here is a list of text error messages that indicate that BIOS could not find a hard drive

- Hard drive not found
- Fixed disk error
- Disk boot failure, insert system disk and press enter

- No boot device available

The problem might be a physical problem with the drive, the data cable, power, or the motherboard. Start with checking BIOS setup to verify that BIOS detected the drive correctly. If the drive was not detected, check the auto detection setting.

A list of error messages that indicate the BIOS was able to find the hard drive but couldn't read what was written on the drive or could not find what it was looking for:
- Invalid boot disk
- Inaccessible boot device
- Invalid drive specification
- Invalid partition table
- No operating system found, Missing operating system, Error loading operating system
- Couldn't find bootmgr or bootmgr is missing (windows vista)
- NTLDR bad or missing (windows XP)
- ➤ For these error messages, you can use **repair or clean installation of windows XP /Vista**. You need to boot from the Windows Vista or windows setup CD, but first check BIOS setup to make sure the boot sequence lists the CD drive before the hard drive.

☞ **Problems at stage 2: after the windows progress bar appears and before logon**
  ✓ **Diagnosis and solution**
When you see the Microsoft progress bar appear during the boot, you know the Windows kernel has loaded successfully and critical drivers and services

configured to be started by the kernel are running. If the progress bar has appeared and the logon screen has not yet been displayed, most likely the problem is caused by a **corrupted driver** or service that is started after the kernel has finished its part of the boot.

> To fix the logon problem you can use safe mode or repair installation of operating system.

☞ **Problems at stage 3: after windows logon**

✓ **Diagnosis and solution**

Problems that occur after the user logs onto Windows are caused by applications or services configured to launch at startup. If you are unable to start Windows normally (after logon), you need to access the Windows Advanced Options menu. This menu is accessed by pressing the F8 key on your keyboard once the POST is completed, and before the Windows splash screen appears.

Once the Windows Advanced Options menu opens, you can choose from the following actions in both Windows XP and Windows Vista:

Safe Mode

Safe Mode with Networking

Safe Mode with Command Prompt

Last Known Good Configuration

Start Windows Normally

Last Known Good Configuration

Last Known Good Configuration is not the first option listed in the Windows Advanced Options menu, but it is usually the first method you should use to try to repair a Windows startup problem. Specifically, Last Known Good

Configuration should be used as the first method of repair if the Windows startup problem began immediately after

- A new device driver was installed
- An update to an existing driver was made
- A new software program was installed

The Last Known Good Configuration option causes Windows to reverse all driver and Registry changes made since the last time you successfully logged on to Windows. This means that if the problem is related to a newly installed driver or program (and you haven't successfully logged on to Windows since the driver or program was installed), you can use Last Known Good Configuration to revert to the original driver or remove the offending program's entries from the Windows Registry.

To initiate Last Known Good Configuration, access the Windows Advanced Options menu, use the arrow keys on your keyboard to scroll down to the Last Known Good Configuration menu item, and press the Enter key. If you are running more than one operating system on your computer, you will need to select the appropriate Windows installation from the menu that appears next. Windows will then attempt to revert to the previous settings, and will automatically restart.

If you are positive that you know which driver or program is causing Windows startup to fail, you may want to bypass the Last Known Good Configuration and go straight to trying to start Windows in Safe mode. That way, you can deal with the specific piece of offending software using Device Manager, or through Add/Remove Programs (Windows XP) or Programs and Features (Windows Vista) in Control Panel. This allows you to deal directly with the rogue driver or software, instead of reversing all the driver and Registry changes made since your last logon.

Starting Windows in Safe Mode

If using Last Known Good Configuration does not solve the Windows startup issue, you should try starting Windows in Safe mode. Using Safe mode gives you the ability to load Windows with only the minimal drivers required to start the core operating system. Starting Windows in Safe mode is sometimes the only way to gain access to a system when the problem is related to a software driver or program.

To start Windows in Safe mode, restart the computer and press and hold the F8 key on the keyboard. This will open the Windows Advanced Options menu. From this menu, you can choose to start Windows in Safe mode, with three different options:

- Safe mode is the standard mode for starting Windows with only the necessary drivers. This is usually the option to choose when you want to start Windows in Safe mode.
- Safe Mode with Networking starts Windows in Safe mode, but includes the drivers necessary for Windows to load its networking components. This can be useful if you want to access online help, but don't have access to another Internet-enabled computer.
- Safe Mode with Command Prompt loads the minimum driver set, and then takes you directly to a command prompt rather than loading the Windows GUI interface.

Note: Starting Windows in Safe mode circumvents a number of drivers and settings. For instance, audio drivers aren't loaded, so you will not have sound when in Safe mode. Also, you will usually not be able to access USB or FireWire devices such as external hard drives. However, you can use USB-based keyboards and mice as long as your computer's firmware supports these devices.

If you are able to start Windows in Safe mode, there are a number of tools you can use to diagnose and solve the problem that is preventing Windows from starting normally.

Device Driver Roll Back
If the Windows startup problem is related to a new or updated device driver (and you are aware of which driver is causing the problem), you can use the Device Driver Roll Back option to revert to the previous version of the driver.

Uninstalling Software through the Windows Control Panel
If the Windows startup problem is related to a recently installed software program, you can remove the offending program after you have started Windows in Safe mode. To do so, open Control Panel in Classic view and double-click on the Add/Remove Programs applet (Windows XP) or the Programs and Features applet (Windows Vista). Select the program you want to uninstall from the list of installed software that appears, and select Remove.

Using the System Restore Tool with Windows XP and Vista
The System Restore tool, which is included in both Windows XP and Windows Vista, can be very useful in recovering a system that has become unreliable for fails to boot properly. The System Restore service monitors the status of certain key files and settings. Every so often, this service takes a

snapshot of certain aspects of your computer's current status. These snapshots are referred to as restore points. You can use the System Restore tool to roll back your machine to one of the recorded restore points.

4.6.2. Troubleshooting running system problems

The Blue Screen of Death: Interpreting STOP Error Messages

Although there are a number of different errors that can occur after Windows XP or Vista has started up, the most damaging and frustrating is the dreaded STOP error, or Blue Screen of Death (BSOD). A STOP error screen can appear during Windows installation, during Windows startup, while you are in the Windows GUI, or even during Windows shutdown.

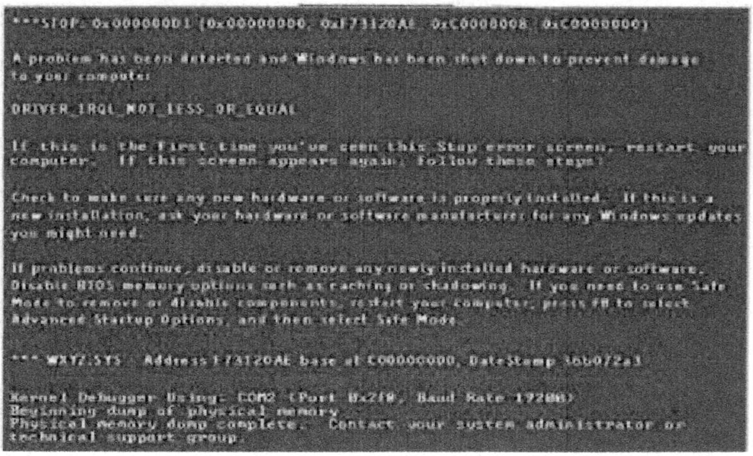

Figure 4.11 Blue Screen of Death

Many things, including **corrupted files, Viruses, incorrectly configured hardware, failing hardware; device driver problems** can cause Windows STOP errors.

Some of the Common stop errors

☞ **STOP: 0x0000000A**

IRQL_NOT_LESS_OR_EQUAL

✓ **Diagnosis & Solution**

This STOP error message is often caused by a **flawed device driver or system firmware.** If the device driver is listed in the STOP error message, try disabling it or rolling back to the previous version.

If this STOP error occurs while you are doing an upgrade installation of Windows XP, you should do a compatibility check of the system by using the Windows XP Upgrade Advisor. This error can also occur if there is antivirus or antispyware software running on the system you are trying to upgrade. Be sure to shut down any instances of these types of software before upgrading a previous version of Windows.

☞ **STOP: 0x0000000A**

IRQL_NOT_LESS_OR_EQUAL

✓ **Diagnosis & Solution**

This STOP error message is often caused by a **flawed device driver or system firmware.** If the device driver is listed in the STOP error message, try disabling it or rolling back to the previous version.

If this STOP error occurs while you are doing an upgrade installation of Windows XP, you should do a compatibility check of the system by using the

111

Windows XP Upgrade Advisor. This error can also occur if there is antivirus or antispyware software running on the system you are trying to upgrade. Be sure to shut down any instances of these types of software before upgrading a previous version of Windows.

☞ STOP: 0x0000007B
INACCESSIBLE_BOOT_DEVICE

✓ **Diagnosis & Solution**

This error is specific to Windows startup. It indicates that Windows was unable to initialize the file system. This could be **caused by a hard drive failure, a damaged hard drive controller, or incorrect settings in the BOOT.INI startup file.**

If all of the hardware is functioning normally, it is still possible that the startup files have become corrupted, or that the Master Boot Record has become damaged. The most common solution this problem is reinstalling operating system.

☞ STOP: 0x000000ED
UNMOUNTABLE_BOOT_VOLUME

✓ **Diagnosis & Solution**

This STOP error occurs when the input/output subsystem fails to mount the boot volume. This can be **due to a damaged file system, but in certain instances can also be caused by a conflict between the disk controller and the hard drive cable.**

If the system uses an Ultra Direct Memory Access (UDMA) controller, and the hard drive is plugged in with a standard 40-wire cable rather than the necessary 80-wire UDMA cable, the end result can be the 0x000000ED UNMOUNTABLE_BOOT_VOLUME STOP error.

However, if the first parameter to appear in parentheses at the top of the STOP error is 0xC0000032, the problem is being caused by a damaged file system. Try using the **CHKDSK /R** command from Recovery Console; if this doesn't solve the problem, try using the **FIXBOOT** command.

Device Driver issue

After formatting your computer with windows XP/vista, some of the devices such as network, printer and sound may not work. This may be due to that the device driver for that hardware or device is not installed or corrupted. In this case you need to install driver software for that particular device.

Note: a device driver is unique for each computer hardware.

Device manger

Device Manager provides an environment for managing hardware devices. Device manager allows you to perform the following types of tasks:

View current device settings

- View the names of the device driver files
- Reconfigure devices

Update device drivers

- Scan for hardware changes
- Remove devices
- Enable or disable devices
- Troubleshoot devices

You can access Device Manager in the following ways (windows XP)

- **In Control Panel**, select Performance and Maintenance, select the System tool, and then, on the Hardware tab of the System Properties dialog box, click the Device manager button.

- **Right-click My Computer and then select Properties**. On the Hardware tab of the System Properties dialog box, click the Device Manager button

- **Right-click My Computer and then select Manage.** Expand the System Tools node and then select Device Manager.

Device Manager uses the following symbols on device icons to denote particular conditions:

- ❖ *Yellow exclamation point* indicates a problem with a device. This could mean that the device has a resource conflict or that Windows is unable to locate the device.

- ❖ *Red "X"* Indicates that the device is disabled.

- ❖ *Blue lowercase "i"* indicates that the device has been configured manually. This icon is viewable only in the Resources by Type and Resources by Connection views.

- ❖ *Yellow question mark* indicates that Windows recognizes that a device is present, but cannot determine the correct device type. This usually means that drivers have not yet been installed for the device.

4.6.3. Running Software Problems

Problems running application software (especially new software) are usually caused by or related to the software itself, or are due to the fact that the software is incompatible with the system. Here is a list of items to check in that case:

- Does the system meet the minimum hardware requirements for the software? Check the soft ware documentation to be sure.
- Check to see that the software is correctly installed. Reinstall if necessary.
- Check to see that the latest drivers are installed.
- Scan the system for malware such as spyware or viruses.

☞ **Applications Don't Install**

These errors generally occur when you're trying to install over an application that already exists, or when you're trying to replace a file that already exists but that another application has in use. When you're installing an application, it is extremely important that you first quit all running programs so the installer can replace any files it needs to.

✓ **Solution**

- Check the program documentation.
- Make sure the program is compatible with Windows version; 16-bit programs (for DOS or Windows 3.x) that need to access hardware directly will not work in 2000 or XP. Newer versions of a program might not run on older versions of Windows.
- Make sure the computer meets the system requirements of the program.
- Copy setup files to the hard drive before running the installation program (usually setup.exe).

☞ **Driver installation unsuccessful**

✓ **Solution**

Try the following:

- Make sure the driver being installed is designed for the installed Windows version.
- Make sure the hardware is compatible with Windows version and with other hardware.
- Make sure the computer meets the system requirements of the hardware (usually printed on the box and in the documentation).
- The device might be malfunctioning. Try the questionable device in another computer or another device in the same computer.

☞ Windows programs stop responding?

A computer, operating system, software program or driver may stop responding or cause other programs to stop responding because of several possible reasons, such as a **confliction of software** or **hardware resources** between two programs, lack of system resources, or a bug in the software or drivers.

✓ Solutions

- Press the CTRL + ALT + DEL keys on his or her keyboards to open the "Close Program" window or open the "**Task Manager**" window and click the "**End Task**" button to terminate the program.

4.7. Review Questions

1. Define the following terms or phrases

    a. Software

    b. Operating system

    c. 32 bit operating system

    d. Multi-boot

2. What are the minimum hardware requirements to install windows 7 Professional?

3. What is the difference between partitioning and formatting?

4. How do u know whether a device or hardware is working properly or not in windows window/7 operating system?

5. How do you disable or enable a hardware or device in windows XP/7 operating system?

6. List the most common pre-windows startup problems. Suggest the possible solutions to fix those problems.

7. What are the most common causes for windows XP/7/8 installation problems?

8. You have inserted windows XP/7/8 installation CD into the CD-ROM drive to perform clean installation but if your computer is not capable of booting from the CD drive, what may be the possible causes for this problem?

Chapter Five

Hardware Troubleshooting

The level of troubleshooting most often performed on PC hardware is exchanging Field Replaceable Units (FRUs). Due to the relative low cost of computer components, it is normally not practical to troubleshoot failed components to the IC level. The cost of using a technician to diagnose the problem further, and repair it, can exceed the cost of the new replacement unit.

5.1. Troubleshooting the CPU

If a PC's processor fails, it can only be replaced. However, most problems that appear to be processor problems are usually a problem with another component. Generally, processor problems fall into three categories:

- Outright failure
- Heating failure
- Compatibility issue.

Outright failure: - if CPU fails, the system fails. You will normally see outright failure as system that refuse to start (not even POST), and crashes that simply cannot be recovered.

Heating failure:-processors run hot, so you need to cool them with some sort of heat sink fun unit. If heat sink is loose or the fan stops, the processor will usually overheat. This often results in a temporary system crash. You must identify and fix heating problems as soon as possible because repeated overheating can destroy the processor.

Compatibility issue:-a motherboard is limited in the number and speed range of processors that it can accommodate. If newly built or upgrade system doesn't boot, verify that the processor is appropriate, and see that the motherboard is configured accordingly.

Here are the most common symptoms that indicate processor failure:
- ➤ The PC will not boot
- ➤ The PC does boot, but will not start the operating system
- ➤ The PC crashes during startup and if it does boot, crashes frequently when running applications
- ➤ The PC restarts by itself after a few minutes of operation

If you experience any of these systems, check the cooling on the processor and on the system, clean the inside of the case, and check the motherboard's power connection.

If a PC boots without problems but consistently halts or freezes after only a few minutes of operation, it is likely that the processor is overheating and shutting itself down. You may need to add a fan or heat sink to the processor or add supplemental cooling fans to the system case. If that is not possible, replace the system case with one that supports multiple system fans.

To troubleshoot the processor, heat sinks, and fan, use the following steps:
(1) Examine the processor's heat sink and fan to verify that they are installed properly and are not cracked or broken.
(2) After making sure the heat sink is not hot, attempt to move it slightly back and forth to check for looseness. If it is loose, it may not have the proper

seal between the heat sink and fan. Follow the directions of the manufacturer to seal the heat sink and fan to the processor.

(3) Remove the heat sink and fan (it typically unclips from the top of the processor) and verify that the processor is properly secured in its socket or slot. If a ZIF (zero insertion force) socket is in use, make sure that the ZIF arm is locked and anchored. Reseat a Slot 1 or Slot A processor package. Reattach the heat sink and fan, making sure it is attached securely and properly.

(4) Make sure that all of the unused expansion slots on the back of the PC's case are filled with slot covers.

If the PC has symptoms of overheating but everything seems to be in order, the problem could be that the system clock jumpers located on the motherboard or the CMOS settings for the system timers are not set correctly for the processor. This would cause the Processor and motherboard to use different clock rates and timings, which would become more out of sync as the system ran and eventually would cause a system failure. Check your motherboard and processor documentation for the proper clock settings and adjust them accordingly.

5.2. Troubleshooting Hard Disk Drives

A hard disk Problem can be caused by

- Incorrect CMOS configuration
- hard disk drive failure
- hard disk controller failure
- drive incompatibility
- cabling problem

- Virus infection

Some things to check when there is hard disk problem:

- **CMOS configuration**: - Check whether BIOS' Startup configuration information stored in CMOS is consistent with what the POST or boot process is finding. Verify the CMOS configuration of each hard disk drive installed in the system.

- **Boot partition files:** - If the system files on the boot partition are corrupted, the system cannot boot properly. If system files are corrupted, Use the CHKDSK command to transfer the system files to the hard drive.
  If this doesn't solve the problem, **reinstall the operating system**. Also verify that the boot partition has not been accidentally removed.

- **Virus infection:** - Another reason the hard disk may not function properly is that the boot disk is infected with a computer virus. Many **viruses can corrupt the master boot record on the hard drive** and cause errors that show up as hard disk errors. If an antivirus program is not installed on the PC, install one and scan the hard disk

- **Hard disk cable connection:-**A message along the lines of "**No hard disk**" indicates that the hard disk is probably installed incorrectly. If the front panel hard drive LED lights up and stays on constantly, the drive data cable is not properly connected. This condition should cause a POST error message indicating that no boot device is available. **Check both ends of the cable**, at the device and on the motherboard or adapter card. Also check the power supply connectors.

- **Hard disk failure:** The hard drive itself may be defective. It can and does happen. Every disk drive makes some noise and users get accustomed to it. However, the spindle motor or the drive bearings can wear out and seize up.

- **Drive incompatibilities-** If two drives will not work with each other in any configuration or combination as master and slave, there is something wrong with the drives or the drives are not compatible with the motherboard. Try replacing one or both and retesting.

- **Hard Disk Controller Failure -**The hard disk controller may be failed, or that the controller is unable to communicate with the attached hard disk. Check the drive cables to see if they are properly connected. Also, check if the hard disk is receiving power, and is spinning up when the system is powered on. If these factors are all accounted for, there may be physical damage to the hard disk, the controller, or the data and/or power cables. Try replacing the data cable first, and if that doesn't solve the problem, try replacing the hard disk. If the error still occurs, it's likely that the disk controller on the motherboard is defective.

5.3. Troubleshooting Optical drives

Most problems with CD and DVD discs are caused by dust, fingerprints, scratches, surface defects, or random electrical noise. Also, a CD or DVD drive will not properly read a CD or DVD when the drive is standing vertically, such as when someone turns a desktop PC case on its side to save desk space.

Use these precautions when handling CDs or DVD:

- Hold the disc by the edge; do not touch the bright side of the disc where data is stored.

- To remove dust or fingerprints, use a clean, soft, dry cloth. Don't wipe the disc in a circular motion.
- Don't paste paper on the surface of a CD. Don't paste any labels on the top of the CD, because this can imbalance the CD and cause the drive to vibrate. You can label a CD using a felt-tip pin. Don't label a DVD if both sides hold data.
- When closing a CD or DVD tray, don't push on the tray. Press the close button on the front of the drive.
- If a disc gets stuck in the drive, use the emergency eject hole to remove it. Turn off the power to the PC first. Then insert an instrument such as a straightened paper clip into the hole to eject the tray manually.

Failure Reading any Disc

If your CD drive fails to read a disc, try the following solutions:

- Check for scratches on the disc data surface.
- Check the drive for dust and dirt; use a cleaning disc.
- Make sure the drive shows up as a working device in System Properties.
- Try a disc that you know works.
- Restart the computer (the magic cure-all).
- Remove the drive from Device Manager in Windows; allow the system to redetect the drive.

Problems when burning a CD

When trying to burn a CD, sometimes Windows refuses to perform the burn or the burned CD is not readable. Here are some things that might go wrong and what to do about them:

- A CD can hold about 700 MB of data. Be sure your total file sizes don't exceed this amount.

- The hard drive needs some temporary holding space for the write process. Make sure you have at least 1 GB of free space.

- If something interrupts the write process before the burning is done, you might end up with a bad CD. Disable any screen saver and close other programs before you begin.

- If several CDs give you problems, try a different brand of CDs

- The burn process requires a constant flow of data to the CD. If you have a sluggish Windows system, a CD might not burn correctly. Try using a slower burn rate to adjust for a slow data transfer rate. To slow the burn rate, right-click the CD-RW drive and select Properties from the shortcut menu. Click the Recording tab and choose a slower write speed from the drop-down menu. Notice in the Recording tab window you can also point to a drive different from drive C to hold temporary files for burning. Use this option if drive C is full, and another drive has more available space.

5.4. Troubleshooting Memory

Typically, three general types of memory (RAM) problems on a PC require troubleshooting, and for the most part, these problems happen just after new memory has been installed. Here below are the three types of problems to check when there is memory problem.

- Configuration problem: If you have just added new or additional memory to a PC, the amount of memory installed may be more than the PC or operating system is able to support or the BIOS CMOS settings may be incorrect.

- Installation problem: Most memory problems are caused by the memory chips or modules not being completely or properly seated in their sockets. It could be that a socket is bad, has a bent or broken lead, or just needs cleaning.

- Hardware problem: All of the memory installed must be compatible and installed in complete banks. If slower memory is installed in one bank, all of the memory will operate at the slower speed. The problem could also be that at least one memory module or chip is defective.

Symptoms of Memory Errors

The following are common instances of memory failures and errors:

➢ **Continuous beep sound:** Clean the memory contacts and reseat the modules. Remove all modules except the first bank. Replace the memory, power supply, and motherboard.

➢ **The PC boots with a blank display:** If the PC is able to boot but the display is blank, it means that an error may have occurred at the beginning of the memory check. The types of conditions to look for are a dislodged expansion card, a memory module not fully seated, or an unsupported memory module. Confirm that all expansion cards and memory modules are seated in their sockets and verify that the memory installed is compatible with the system by checking its part numbers.

➢ **The memory count displayed by the POST is wrong:** A wrong memory type being installed is a common cause for his error, as well as memory banks not being completed. Another problem is incompatible memory or more memory than the system is able to address.

➢ **The PC displays a memory error message**, such as:

✓ Memory mismatch error

✓ Memory parity interrupt at nnnnn

✓ Memory address error at nnnnn

✓ Memory failure at nnnnn, read nnnnn, expecting nnnnn

These errors typically point out problems **between old memory and new memory Or a failing memory module**. If removing a newly installed memory module eliminates the error, replace the old memory with the new memory .If the error shows up again, the new memory is either defective or not compatible with the system. Another cause for these messages can be a motherboard problem.

➢ **Intermittent memory problems:** these are problems that show up sporadically as an error message, system crash, or a spontaneous system reboot. The causes for this problem are ESD (electrostatic discharge), overheating, or a faulty power supply.

➢ **Software-related memory problems:** The problems under this category include registry errors, general-protection and page faults, and exception errors. Registry errors happen when the Windows operating system writes parts of the registry to a defective portion of RAM. Software bugs cause faults and exception errors. For example, an application may release its memory when completed or it may try to occupy the same memory address as another. Rebooting the PC usually solves these problems.

5.5. Motherboard Troubleshooting

When you're troubleshooting a computer, there is no shortage of places to look for problems. However, because the motherboard is the "home" for the most essential system resources, it's often the source of many problems. If you see the following problems, consider the motherboard as a likely place to look for the cause:

- **System won't start**— when you push the power button on an ATX or BTX system, the computer should start immediately. If it doesn't, the problem could be motherboard–related.

- **Devices connected to the port cluster don't work**— If ports in the port cluster are damaged or disabled in the system BIOS configuration (CMOS setup), any devices connected to the port cluster will not work.

- **Mass storage drives are not recognized or do not work**— If mass storage ports on the motherboard are not properly connected to devices, are disabled, or are not configured properly, drives connected to these ports will not work.

- **Memory failures**— Memory failures could be caused by the modules themselves, or they could be caused by the motherboard.

System won't start: detail explanation

If the computer will not start, check the following:

- Incorrect front panel wiring connections to the motherboard
- Loose or missing power leads from power supply
- Loose or missing memory modules
- Loose BIOS chips
- Dead short in system

The following sections describe each of these possible problems.

Incorrect Front Panel Wiring Connections to the Motherboard: The power switch is wired to the motherboard, which in turn signals the power supply to start. If the power lead is plugged into the wrong pins on the motherboard, or has been disconnected from the motherboard, the system will not start and you will not see an error message.

Check the markings on the front panel connectors, the motherboard, or the motherboard/system manual to determine the correct pin outs and installation.

Loose or Missing Power Leads from Power Supply: Modern power supplies often have both a 20- or 24-pin connection and a four- or eight-pin connection to the motherboard. If either or both connections are loose or not present, the system cannot start and you will not see an error message.

Loose or Missing Memory Modules: If the motherboard is unable to recognize any system memory, it will not start properly. Unlike the other problems, you will see a memory error message.

Loose BIOS Chips: Socketed motherboard chips that don't have retaining mechanisms, such as BIOS chips, can cause system failures if the chips work loose from their sockets. The motherboard BIOS chip is responsible for displaying boot errors, and if it is not properly mounted in its socket, the system cannot start and no error messages will be produced (note that many recent systems have surface-mounted BIOS chips).

Dead Short (Short Circuit) in System: A dead short (short circuit) in your system will prevent a computer from showing any signs of life when you turn it on. Some of the main causes for dead shorts that involve motherboards include

- **Incorrect positioning of a standoff**: - Standoffs, also called spacers, are round plastic or metal pegs that separate the motherboard from the

128

case, so that components on the back of the motherboard do not touch the case. Make sure the locations of the standoffs match the screw holes on the motherboard. Some motherboards have two types of holes: plain holes that are not intended for use with brass standoffs (they might be used for heat sink mounting or for plastic standoffs) and reinforced holes used for brass standoffs. If a brass standoff is under a part of the motherboard not meant for mounting, such as under a plain hole or under the solder connections, the standoff could cause a dead short that prevents the system from starting.

- **Loose screws or slot covers**: - Leaving a loose screw inside the system and failing to fasten a slot cover or card in place are two common causes for dead shorts, because if these metal parts touch live components on the motherboard, your system will short out and stop working.

5.6. Review Questions

1. What are the Hard disk drive interfaces?

2. What are the most common causes for hard disk problem?

3. What is the use of partitioning a hard drive?   List two advantages

4. You've installed one IDE/SATA hard drive, and it is working fine. You install a second IDE/SATA drive, and neither drives works when you start the system. What is the most likely cause for this problem?

5. What symptoms point to the need of more RAM in a PC?

6. If your motherboard supports memory module 200 pin, will 240 pin memories still work on the board?

7. You have been asked to install a SATA hard drive containing important data into a system with an older (IDE) motherboard that does not have SATA connections. Is this possible? If so, what is the best way to do it?

Chapter Six

Securing Computer Resources

6.1. Security threats

Protecting and securing your computer is a major concern with the growing number of malicious software applications circulating on the Internet. The following are two major security threats for a computer system.

6.1.1. Unauthorized people

People that use your computer or obtaining the information you have in it, either by probing it physically, or by probing it with software through a network or the Internet.

Preventing unauthorized people from using your computer

Physically protecting your computer and data might be one of the security measures you implement. Here are some suggestions:

- **Password protect**: - Assign strong password for each of the accounts on your computer.

- **If your data is really private, keep it under lock and key**: - You can use all kinds of security methods to encrypt, password protect, and hide data, but if it really is that important, one obvious thing you can do is store the data on a removable storage device such as a flash drive and, when you're not using the data, put the flash drive in a fireproof safe. You can also use folder lock software to protect your folders and files. Folder lock is a **full-suite data security solution** for Windows 7, Windows Vista and Windows XP. Folder Lock lets you lock, hide and password-protect files, folders and drives with a simple drag and drop;

encrypt your important files; optionally backup and sync those encrypted files in real-time, and store them to any portable device. You can get folder lock software freely from the internet.

- **Lock down the computer case**: - Some computer cases allow you to add a lock so that you can physically prevent others from opening the case.

- **Using encryption techniques:** - Encryption puts data into code that must be translated before it can be accessed, and can be applied in several ways. Please read the notes or steps from internet on how to encrypt a folder or file.

Using Windows Passwords

Passwords are your first line of defense for both local and remote attacks on your computer. If you do not already have a password assigned to all of the accounts on your computer, it is very easy to set it up. Just open the Control Panel and click on User Accounts. Then click on the name of the account and click the Create Password button. To set a password for a user, right-click on the name of the account and select Set Password.

Recovering a Lost Password

Forgetting a password to an account on your computer can be very frustrating. There are different methods to recover your forgotten window password. You can use one of the following methods depending on your need.

Control userpasswords2:-If you know one of the administrator user account password on your computer then you can log in with that account and then type **control userpasswords2** from run command. From there, you can right-click on any account and reset its password.

Password reset disk:-If you do not remember any administrator password, the only feasible way to get into an account that you forgot the password is to use password reset disk to essentially overwrite the specific account's password data.

6.1.2. Malware (bad and undesired software)

Having getting installed on your computer, malwares will take advantage of you and your Internet connection to do things you don't want. Malware comes in many forms, including:

- **Viruses** that may infect all of the documents on your computer and may even erase or corrupt critical operating system files.

- **Spyware** is software that installs itself on your computer to spy on you and to collect personal information about you that it transmits over the Internet to Web-hosting sites. These sites might use your personal data in harmless or harmful ways such as tailoring marketing information to suit your shopping habits, tracking marketing trends, or stealing your identity for harm. Spyware comes to you by way of e-mail attachments, downloaded freeware or shareware, instant messaging programs, or when you click a link on a malicious Web site.

- **Adware** produces all those unwanted pop-up ads. Adware is secretly installed on your computer when you download and install shareware or freeware, including screen savers, desktop wallpaper, music, cartoons, news, and weather alerts. Then it displays pop-up ads which might be based on your browsing habits.

- **Spam** is junk e-mail that you don't want, you didn't ask for, and that gets in your way.

Computer virus

A computer virus is a program that replicates itself to other computers, generally causing those computers to behave abnormally. A virus's main function is to reproduce and attaches itself to files on a hard disk and modifies those files.

Types of viruses

Viruses can classified into different types based on origin, techniques, types of files they infect, where they hide, the kind of damage they cause, the type of operating system or platform they attack. The following are common types of viruses.

- **Boot sector Virus**: - can hide in either of two boot sectors of a hard drive.
- **A file virus:** - hides in an executable program having an .exe, .com, .sys, .vbs, or other executable file extension, or in a word-processing document that contains a macro.
- **A multipartite virus:**- is a combination of a boot sector virus and a file virus and can hide in either.
- **Macro viruses:** - are the most common viruses spread by e-mail, hiding in macros of attached document files.

Common symptoms of computer viruses

- Your computer runs more slowly than normal
- Your computer stops responding or locks up often
- Your computer crashes and restarts every few minutes
- Your computer restarts on its own and then fails to run normally
- Applications on your computer don't work correctly

- Disks or disk drives are inaccessible
- You can't print correctly
- You see unusual error messages
- You see distorted menus and dialog boxes
- Your antivirus software displays one or more messages.

Spyware

Spyware is software that can install itself or run on your computer without providing you with adequate notice, consent, or control. Spyware might not display symptoms after it infects your computer, but many types of spyware or unwanted programs can affect how your computer runs. For example, spyware can monitor your online behavior or collect information about you (including personally identifiable or other sensitive information), change settings on your computer, or cause your computer to run slowly.

Common symptoms of spyware or unwanted software

You probably have some form of spyware on your computer if:

- You notice new toolbars, links, or favorites that you didn't intentionally add to your web browser.
- Your default home page, mouse pointer, or search program changes.
- You type the address for a specific website (for example, a search engine), but are taken to another website without notice.
- You see pop-up ads, even if you're not on the Internet.
- Your computer suddenly begins to start or run slowly.

There might be spyware on your computer even if you don't see any symptoms. This type of software can collect information about you and your computer without your knowledge or consent

Protecting against malicious software

Malicious software, also called **malware**, or a computer **infestation**, is any unwanted program that harm and is transmitted to your computer without your knowledge.

- **Use antivirus (AV) software**. As a defensive and offensive measure to protect against malicious software, install and run antivirus (AV) software and keep it current. Configure the AV software so that it automatically downloads updates to the software and runs in the background.

- **Always use a software firewall**. Never, ever connect your computer to an unprotected network without using a firewall. Recall that Windows Firewall can be configured to allow no uninvited communication in or to allow in the exceptions that you specify.

- **Limit the use of administrator accounts**. If malware installs itself while you're logged on as an administrator, it will most likely be running under this account with more privileges and the ability to do more damage than if you had been logged on under a less powerful account. Use an account with lesser privileges for your everyday normal computer activities.

- **Set Internet Explorer for optimum security**. Internet Explorer includes the pop-up blocker, the ability to manage add-ons, the ability to block scripts and disable scripts embedded in Web pages, and the ability to set the general security level. For most Web browsing, set the security level to Medium-high, also consider updating IE to the latest version because later versions are likely to have enhanced security features.

- **Use alternate client software**. Using alternate client software, including browsers and email clients, can give you an added layer of protection from malicious software that targets Microsoft products. Firefox by Mozilla (www.mozilla.org) is an excellent browser, and Thunderbird, also by Mozilla, is a popular e-mail client. Some people even use a different OS than Windows because of security issues.

- **Keep good backups**. One of the more important chores of securing a computer is to prepare in advance for disaster to strike. One of the most important things you can do to prepare for disaster is to make good backups of user data.

6.2. Review Questions

1. What are the major security threats for a computer system?
2. How do you know whether your computer is infected with virus?
3. How can I tell if I have spyware or unwanted software on my computer?
4. How can I prevent spyware or virus from infecting my computer?

Chapter Seven

Windows Built-in Troubleshooting Tools

There are several tools and settings useful when dealing with Windows problems that occur after startup. Windows XP, Vista and 7 include a number of built-in tools and resources for troubleshooting minor errors that occur within the operating system. Some of these troubleshooting tools and resources can be grouped as follows:-

7.1. Tools used for troubleshooting minor errors

☞ CHKDSK

Use CHKDSK to check and repair errors on a volume or logical drive. If critical system files are affected by these errors, repairing the drive might solve a startup problem. CHKDSK can be used as a command-line tool, or is available through the Windows GUI (although the GUI version doesn't include all the functionality of the command-line version).

Here is a list of the switches you can use with CHKDSK for Windows XP and Vista:

/f   CHKDSK attempts to fix any errors that it finds.

/r   CHKDSK attempts to locate bad sectors and recover any readable data from them.

/v   On a FAT or FAT32 file system volume, CHKDSK will display the name and full path of every file on the disk. On an NTFS volume, this switch displays relevant information on any actions CHKDSK performs.

Example: To check drive C: and repair it:

C:\> Chkdsk C: /r

There is a version of CHKDSK you can run from within the Windows GUI (graphical user interface).

To open CHKDSK

Double-click My Computer or select it from the Start Menu and right-click on the volume or drive (e.g. local disk C) you want to scan. Click Properties, select the Tools tab, and click Check Now.

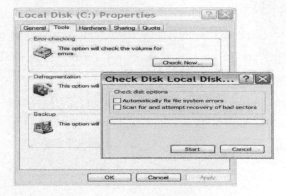

Figure 7.1 Running the GUI version of CHKDSK while Windows is running.

Program Compatibility Wizard

- Is used as a workaround for compatibility issues with a program that was released for an earlier version of Windows that has trouble functioning under Windows XP.
- The Program Compatibility Wizard can be launched from the Start menu by choosing All Programs, Accessories. Alternatively, you can

139

right-click on a program's launch file or shortcut, select Properties, and then click on the Compatibility tab.

- You can choose to run a program in one of the following Windows compatibility modes for Windows **95, 98, Me, NT4.0 (SP5), and 2000.** The Program Compatibility Wizard also offers three display options for older programs:

  ✓ Run in 256 Colors

  ✓ Run in 640x480 Screen Resolution

  ✓ Disable Visual Themes

System File Checker (Sfc.exe)

- At a command prompt, enter SfcChecker (Sfc.exe) with parameters.
- Use it to verify the version of all system files when Windows loads. Useful when you suspect system files are corrupted, but you can still access the Windows desktop.

Task Manager (Taskman.exe)

- Right-click the taskbar and select (Taskman.exe) Task Manager.
- Use it to list and stop currently running processes. Useful when you need to stop a locked-up application.

7.2. Tools used for increasing PC performance

Disk clean up

Hard disk is full of trash. You never see that a window keeps for you. Here are a few examples.

- Files in the recycle bin: temporally deleted files
- Temporary internet Files: when you are using internet.

- Downloaded Program files: your system always keeps a copy of any Java ActiveX applets that it downloads.
- Temporary Files: many applications create temporary files that are supposed to be deleted when the application closed. For one reason or the other these temporary files are not deleted. The locations of these files are always resided in a folder called TEMP.

Removing these unnecessary files has a great roll on the speed of the computer. To do so, follow the following steps.

- open My computer , right click on the drive(partition) ,Click properties , Click General tab, Click Disk Clean Up Button

    Or

- Start→programs→accessories→system tools disk clean up

Disk Defragmenter

✓ Information stored on hard drives using the Windows file systems FAT 32 and NTFS are prone to file fragmentation.

✓ As data are added to the drive, they are written sequentially on the drive platters; as information is accessed and edited, however, parts of the files are moved out of sequence.

✓ Defragmenting the drive improves read performance / computer performance.

Steps to defrag hard disk:

(1) Click Start _ My Computer

(2) Right-click the drive you want to defrag, which will most likely be the C drive

(3) Select Properties

(4) The Local Disk (C :) Properties box will open. Click the Tools tab

(5) Under Defragmentation, click the Defragment Now button

(6) Click Analyze

7.3. Tools used for getting PC information

These are the most common tools used for getting information about a particular computer.

- System Information(Msinfo32.exe)
- DirectX Diagnostic Tool (dxdiag)
- Device manager (Devmgmt.msc)

System Information (Msinfo32.exe)

Use system information to display information about hardware, applications, and Windows. System Information collects system information, such as devices that are installed in your computer, device drivers that are loaded in your computer and provides a menu for displaying the associated system topics. The System Summary category provides a general profile of your computer. This information includes:

- The version of Windows
- OEM System Information (manufacturer, model, and type)
- The type of central processing unit (CPU)
- The amount of memory and system resources
- BIOS version
- Locale
- Time zone
- computer is configured to log into a domain)
- Boot device (if multiple devices are present on the computer)
- The path to the Page file

To start Microsoft System Information, use either of the following methods

1. Click Start, point to Programs, point to Accessories, point to System Tools, and then click System Information. Or

2. Click Start, click Run, type **msinfo32.exe** in the Open box, and then click OK.

DirectX Diagnostic Tool (DXDIAG.EXE)

- DirectX Diagnostic Tool displays information regarding the various DirectX-related drivers, and provides a series of user-initiated diagnostic tests you can use to determine if DirectX and the hardware devices it interacts with are functioning normally.

- To launch it, go to the Start menu, select Run, and type DXDIAG.EXE.

Device manager

Device Manager provides a graphical view of the hardware that is installed on the computer, as well as the device drivers and resources associated with that hardware.

To access Device Manager, use any of the following methods:

- Click Start, click Run, and then type devmgmt.msc. or

- Right-click My Computer, click Manage, and then click Device Manager. Or

- Right-click My Computer, click Properties, click the Hardware tab, and then click Device Manager.

Device Manager allows the following functionality

- Determine if the hardware on your computer is working properly.

- Change hardware configuration settings.

143

- Identify the device drivers that are loaded for each device and obtain information about each device driver.
- Change advanced settings and properties for devices.
- Install updated device drivers.
- Disable, enable, and uninstall devices.
- Reinstall the previous version of a driver.
- Identify device conflicts and manually configure resource settings.
- Print a summary of the devices that are installed on your computer.

Working with device manager

After you get the device manager a list of devices appears.

- If a device has problems, the device has a red cross(X) point next to it(i.e. disabled device)
- If a device is unknown (usually because of **missing drivers**), the device has a yellow question mark (?) next to it.

7.3. Tools for fixing start up problems

System Configuration Utility (msconfig.exe)

- This utility is used for temporarily disabling startup programs and services.
- To access the System Configuration Utility from the Start menu, select Run, and enter MSCONFIG.

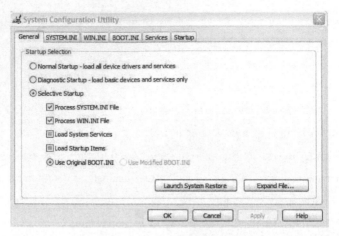

Figure 7.2 Using **msconfig.exe** to manually set startup variables

Safe mode

- At startup, press **F8** and select the option from the Advanced Boot Options menu.

- Use it when Windows does not start or starts with errors. Safe Mode loads the Windows desktop with a minimum configuration. In this minimized environment, you can solve a problem with a device driver, display setting, or corrupted or malicious applications.

7.4. Tools for removing unwanted software

Add or remove program

- Use it to uninstall, repair, or update software or certain device drivers that are causing a problem.

- Accessed from Control Panel.

Malicious software removal tool (MRT.exe)

Microsoft offers the Malicious Software Removal Tool, which is updated once a month. The tool scans your computer for most new viruses and malicious software. After you run the tool, you will get a report that describes any malicious software found on your computer and lists all the viruses it scanned for.

To start malicious software removal tool

Click on start→run→type **mrt.exe**→ok

7.5. **Tools used for solving other problems**

Systems restore

Use it to restore the system to a previously working condition; it restores the registry, some system files, and some application files.

Steps to open system restore:

Click Start → Programs → Accessories→ System Tools → System Restore

Back up

- To help ensure that you don't lose your files, you should back them up regularly. You can set up automatic backups or manually back up your files at any time.
- Enter Ntbackup.exe in the XP Run dialog box or start—program--accessories—system tools---back up
- For vista and window 7 , start-- control panel--system and security---backup and restore

Driver Signing and Digital Signatures (Sigverif.exe)

- At a command prompt, enter **Sigverif** with parameters.

146

- When a device driver or other software is giving problems, use it to verify that the software has been approved by Microsoft.

Memory Diagnostics (mdsched.exe)

- Enter **mdsched.exe** in a command prompt window.

- Use it to test memory.

Event Viewer

- Accessed from the Computer Management console.

- Check the Event Viewer logs for error messages to help you investigate all kinds of hardware, security, and system problems.

Registry Editor (Regedit.exe)

- The registry is a database in Windows that contains important information about system hardware, installed programs and settings, and profiles of each of the user accounts on your computer. Windows continually refers to the information in the registry.

- Before you make changes to a registry key or subkey, I recommend that you export, or make a backup copy, of the key or subkey. You can save the backup copy to a location you specify, such as a folder on your hard disk or a removable storage device

- To access registry, at a command prompt, enter Regedit.

- Use it to view and edit the registry

7.4. Review Questions

1. What are the windows built in tools used for troubleshooting minor errors?
2. What is the function of task manager?
3. When do you use disk clean up?
4. When do you use disk Defragmenter?
5. How do you know general information such as RAM size, processor speed and hard disk size in your computer?
6. What are the most common window XP/7/8 tools used to fix start up problems?
7. What is the function of safe mode?
8. When do you use system restore?

Chapter Eight

PC maintenance, Diagnostics and Troubleshooting

8.1. Preventive maintenance

Preventive maintenance is a service given for the purpose of maintaining equipments and facilities in satisfactory operating conditions by providing systematic inspection detection and correction of failures either before they occur or before they develop into major defects. Preventive maintenance can prevent certain computer problems from occurring in the first place. The more preventive maintenance work you do initially, the fewer problems you are likely to have later, and the less troubleshooting and repair you will have to do.

Advantage of preventive maintenance

Preventive maintenance has the following long term benefits:

- Improves system reliability
- Decreases cost of replacement
- Decreases system downtime

The following are common tips for preventive maintenance:

- **Physically inspect the computer by doing the following:**
  - Make sure the computer is in a proper environment.
  - Check that air vents on the computer case or monitor are not blocked by papers, books, drapes, or other obstructions.
  - Make sure the inside of the computer case is free from dust. Use an antistatic vacuum, blower, or can of compressed air to blow the dust out of the case and clean vents, power supply, and fans.
  - Verify that chips and expansion cards are firmly seated.

149

- Clean the keyboard. Unplug the keyboard and then blow or vacuum it out.
- Clean the mouse. To clean a wheel mouse, remove the cover of the mouse ball from the bottom of the mouse. The cover usually comes off with a simple press and shifts or turn motion.
- Clean the screen with a lint-free cloth. You can also use special monitor wipes that are safe for CRT and LCD monitors.

- Verify that antivirus software is installed, running, and updated.
- Always use the **Shut Down option** to close the Windows operating system before powering down the PC.
- **Never connect or disconnect** a serial, parallel, or video device while the system is running.
- **Antistatic wrist or ankle strap-** Always wear Antistatic wrist strap when working inside the system unit (case) to avoid possible damage from electrostatic discharge (ESD).
- **UPS or surge protector-** Verify the system is protected against electrical surges or spikes by using a UPS or surge protector.
- **Backup of data** - If the computer is used to hold important data, verify data is being backed up on a regular basis and backup media is being kept in an offsite location.
- **Defragmenting the drive-** Rearrange noncontiguous parts of files, delete unneeded files, and check the drive for errors.
- **Disk clean up-** To keep Windows from starting slowly, reduce Windows startup programs to a minimum and delete temporary files and check the hard drive for errors.

8.2. PC Diagnostics

Diagnosis is way of listing the cause of the problem by considering different things. Trial and error isn't the only way to diagnose a problem. Many hardware- and software-based tools exist to let you know what is wrong. In my experience, search engines such as Google are also the most important tools to solve computer problems.

Here are some diagnostic tools that can be very helpful in isolating defective hardware components.

- POST
- Hiren's BootCD
- Ubuntu Live CD
- POST card
- Multimeter
- Software diagnostic packages

POST (Power-On Self Test)

The power-on self test runs whenever a PC is turned on. POST is a series of program routines buried in the motherboard ROM-BIOS chip that tests all the main system components at power-on time. This series of routines is partially responsible for the delay when you turn on your PC; the computer executes the POST before loading the operating system. It checks the primary components in your system, such as the CPU, ROM, and motherboard support circuitry, memory, and major peripherals such as the expansion chassis. The POST process provides error or warning messages whenever it encounters a faulty component. If the POST encounters a problem severe enough to keep the system from operating properly, it halts the system boot process and generates an error message that often identifies the cause of the problem.

The POST tests normally provide three types of output messages: audio codes, onscreen text messages, and hexadecimal numeric codes that are sent to an input/output port address. POST errors can be displayed in the following three ways:

Hiren's BootCD

Hiren's BootCD is an impressive toolkit rolled into one packed DOS-based Live CD. Sporting over a hundred separate diagnostic and repair tools, Hiren's BootCD can help you do everything from diagnose a memory problem to clone a disk to speed test your video card.

Hiren's BootCD contains the following tools.

Partition Tools: You can both create and delete partitions from your computer, even while there are other partitions on the hard drive you are modifying. Also you can resize partitions if needed, to change how much space is allocated to them.

Backup and Recovery: There are installments backup and recovery tools on Hiren's BootCD. You copy data off of your hard drive and schedule automatic backups to ensure your data is saved to another location. Also you can recover deleted data, whether that data was deleted intentionally or accidentally. There Are Also A Few tools that will of help you recover data from Damaged or corrupted portions of your hard drive if you are Unable to recover them through other methods.

Testing Tools: Hiren's BootCD provides a variety of tools for testing different aspects of your computer. That if you suspect your RAM is

152

corrupted or that a piece of hardware on your machine is not functioning properly, there are installments can applications you run to determine the problems.

Password Tools: Password recovery and modification tools are also provided on Hiren's BootCD. You can change the administrator password on Windows machines, and there are utilities for saving passwords for your online accounts in an encrypted format. Also you can encrypt your entire hard drive with Hiren's BootCD so That a password is required to read or write any data from or to your hard drive.

Ubuntu Live CD

You can use an Ubuntu Live CD to test your computer's memory, recover data, or scan your computer for viruses. Live CDs are great for giving you a platform to work independently of your troubled system. Boot up your computer with a Ubuntu Live CD or USB drive. You will be greeted with this screen:

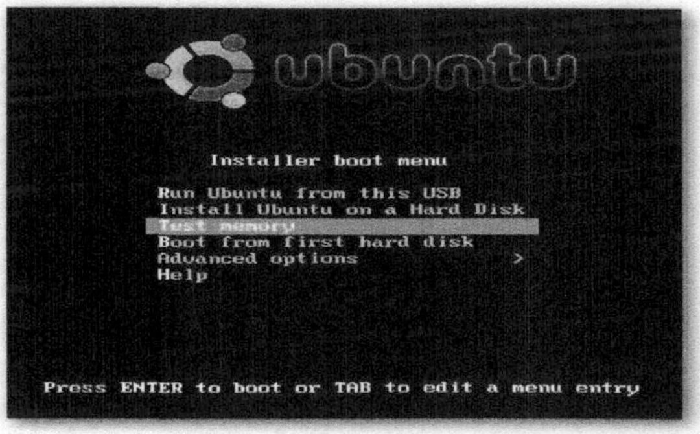

Figure 8.1 Ubuntu live CD

Use the down arrow key to select the Test memory option and hit Enter. Memtest86+ will immediately start testing your RAM.

POST Card

POST card is a diagnostic device that plugs into the system's expansion slot and tests the operation of the system as it boots up. POST cards are normally used when the system appears to be dead, or when the system cannot read from a floppy or hard drive. If at least the CPU, BIOS, and the I/O interface the POST card relies on are working, the system sends two-hexadecimal-digit codes to a specified I/O port (usually 80 hex) during startup, some indicating a stage in the startup procedure, others identifying errors.

Multimeter

A multimeter or a multitester, also known as a VOM (Volt-Ohm meter), is an electronic measuring instrument that combines several measurement functions in one unit. A typical multimeter may include features such as the ability to measure voltage, current and resistance. Multimeters may use analog or digital circuits—analog multimeters (AMM) and digital multimeters (often abbreviated DMM or DVOM). You can use a multimeter when a PC won't power on, there are many possible causes, such as a bad cable, faulty switch, or blown power supply. A multimeter can help you find the cause of your particular problem quickly and easily. With this tool, you can perform **continuity tests** on cables and switches and test the voltage on the **power supply**. Please read other references for more information on how to use multimeter.

Software Diagnostic Packages

Several commercially available disk-based diagnostic routines can check the system by running predetermined tests on different areas of its hardware. The diagnostic package evaluates the   response from each test and attempts to produce a status report for all of the system's major components. The most common software-troubleshooting packages test the system's memory, microprocessor, keyboard, display monitor, and the disk drive's speed. If at least the system's CPU, disk drive, and clock circuits are working, you might be able to use one of these special software-troubleshooting packages to help localize system failures.

8.3. Common hardware problems and their solutions

☞ **Problem**

No Power light appears on the Computer (Monitor and System Unit) and

There is no display on the screen.

✓ **Solution**

- Check the power line from the wall outlet.
- Check the adapter sockets.
- Check the power cables.
- Check that the system unit's power supply is plugged into the wall outlet (adapter socket)
- Check that the monitor is plugged into the wall outlet (adapter socket).
- Check the system unit's ON\ OFF switch.
- Check the monitor's ON\OFF switch.

☞ **Problem**

System unit's power lights, fan sound and no power light on the monitor.

✓ **Solution**

- Check the monitor power connection.
- Use the replacement method.

☞ **Problem**

Both the monitor's and the system unit's power lights but no picture on the screen.

✓ **Solution**

- Note: The red power light on the monitor indicates 'no signal' has been sent to the monitor through the monitor's data cable, and the green light indicates: that the monitor has received a signal from the CPU.
- Check if the monitor brightness and contrast is on accurate setting.
- Re-attach the data cable. The data (video) cable that connects the monitor to the video card may be unplugged.

☞ **Problem**

Still the monitor and computer system Power lights came on but there is no picture on the screen.

✓ **Solution**

- Reseat the video card firmly. [Don't forget ESD]
- The video cable (pins) might fail. [So check it]
- The video card might fail. [Replace it]
- The monitor might fail.

• Use the replacement method.

☞ **Problem**

The PC beeps normal but there is no display

✓ **Solution**

- Make sure the monitor has power
- Check the connection to the video card
- Check the Video Card

☞ **Problem**

When I turn the PC on, it starts up but never loads the operating system

✓ **Solution**

- Check the Hard Disk
- Check the Memory
- Check the Motherboard
- Check the CPU

☞ **Problem**

While the system is on and working, it shuts itself off

(Restart after some minutes)

✓ **Solution**

- Check the power features in the BIOS
- Check the power features in the Windows Control Panel
- Check the Power Supply
- Check that all fans are working
- Check for the accumulation of dust

☞ **Problem**

I can't hear any sound from the speakers

✓ **Solution**

- Change the CD
- Still there is no sound – Try to play different file type (e.g:MP3)
- Check whether your computer plays system sounds. System sounds are the sounds that are already available in your system OS.
- Check the volume control to see that they are turned up and not muted
- Check whether the speakers connected properly
- Check for hardware conflicts and devices that are turned off
- Check whether the sound card is defective or not

8.4. Troubleshooting methods

Troubleshooting is the process of identifying a computer problem so that it can be fixed. Every computer users has his or her own way to troubleshoot. Some people use their instincts while others need an advice from other people. But let us see common troubleshooting methods.

1. Gather information

Ask the customer the following questions to define the problems:

- Can you tell me something about the problem?
- What did you do to your computer lastly [Before it stopped working]?
- How often does this happen? Have you installed new software Have you deleted some files?
- Have you added a new hardware device?

158

- Have you made any other changes to the computer recently?

2. **Check the power and cable connectors**

   - Check the power line.
   - Check the wall outlet power.
   - Check the power sockets.
   - Check the cables.
   - Is it plugged in?
   - Is it turned on?
   - Is the computer ready to accept command from the user?
   - Open the case covers and Reset chips and cables.

3. **Check if the error is user's error**

   - Because the user cannot print.
   - Because the user cannot save the files
   - Because the user cannot run application etc.
   - If the user is wrong, show him/her how to use the computer.

4. **Restart the computer**

This process is called a "cold boot" (since the machine was off or cold when it started). A "warm boot" is the same except it occurs when the machine is rebooted using {CTRL+ALT+DELETE}.

Note: Reboot can solve or show the problem. Rebooting doesn't work, try to power down the system completely, and then power it up

5. **Define if the problem is a hardware or software related**

   - Is it a startup problem?
   - Is it windows problem?
   - Is it a program problem?

- Is it a device problem?

6. Find out the problem and solve it!

- If the problem is hardware related, determine which component is failing and try to solve the problem.
- If the problem is software related; determine which is corrupted or missed and try to solve the problem.

8.5.   Review Questions

1. What is preventive maintenance?
2. What is the difference between maintenance and troubleshooting?
3. What is the advantage of preventive maintenance?
4. What are diagnostic tools that can be very helpful in isolating defective hardware components?
5. If you forget your window 7 administrator account password, how do you reset the password without installing the window?
6. How do you use Ubuntu Live CD as a diagnostic tool?

Chapter Nine

Data Backup and Recovery

9.1. Data Backup

Data Backup is the physical copying of data files to a removable storage device that allows the data to be stored in another location. When needed, an individual data file or an entire set of data files, can be restored to a computer system. Maintaining a good set of backups is a critical part of preventative maintenance.

Advantages of Backup

Files can be lost from your computer in any number of ways. You might accidentally delete a file, or a virus might wipe one out. You can also have a complete hard drive failure. When a hard drive dies, it's kind of like having your house burn down. Important personal items are usually gone forever— family photos, significant documents, downloaded music, and more. Therefore, it is important to back up your files to a second, separate location. By doing so, your files can be protected against viruses or complete computer failure.

Tips for Data Backup

- There are many ways to backup data on your computer - the least effective of which (for obvious reasons) is having the only backup location on your actual hard drive. Instead, use external hardware such as a disk, CD, zip drive, or memory stick.

- Online backup is another option. This requires the use of an Internet-based data backup storage service.

161

- If space on your computer is limited, be selective with the data you choose to backup. For example, you may choose to only backup personal data. As a general rule, there's no need to backup entire programs, as in the event that they are deleted, you can simply reinstall them with original software. For this reason, it's important to keep a copy of your operating system on hand.

Backup data before formatting a computer

There are many reasons why you need to format your hard drive. You may be installing a new Operating System, or simply clean your system to remove viruses and spyware, or to clear the drive if you're selling the drive, and more. But before you format the hard drive, you must perform the following tasks.

1. Back up all important data from your hard drive
2. Make sure you have the Operating System Disk with you and all important software you want to install after you finish formatting
3. Make sure you check which drive you are formatting and be careful when you re-arrange or create your partitions.

How to back up your files in window 7

To help ensure that you don't lose your files, you should back them up regularly. You can set up automatic backups or manually back up your files at any time using the following steps.

1. Open Backup and Restore by clicking the Start button, clicking Control Panel, clicking System and Maintenance, and then clicking Backup and Restore.
2. Do one of the following:
   - If you've never used Windows Backup before, click Set up backup, and then follow the steps in the wizard. If you're prompted for an

administrator password or confirmation, type the password or provide confirmation.

- If you've created a backup before, you can wait for your regularly scheduled backup to occur, or you can manually create a new backup by clicking back up now. If you're prompted for an administrator password or confirmation, type the password or provide confirmation.

9.2. Recovering deleted Files

Recovering files within the recycle bin

The Recycle Bin provides protection against accidental erasure of files. In most cases, when you delete one or more files or folders, the deleted items go to the Recycle Bin. To retrieve a file from the Recycle Bin, open the Recycle Bin, select the file, right-click it, and select Restore. Windows lists the file in its original location and removes it from the Recycle Bin.

The following kinds of deletions do not go to the Recycle Bin:

- Files stored on removable disks
- Files stored on network drives, even when that volume is on a computer that has its own Recycle Bin
- Files deleted from a command prompt
- Files deleted from compressed (zipped) folders

If you hold down the Shift key when you select Delete or press the Delete key, the Recycle Bin is bypassed. Retrieving lost data at this point requires third-party data recovery software.

Recovering files that are not in the recycle bin

Third-party softwares are necessary if you want to retrieve files that are not in the recycle bin or to recover files that are deleted permanently from your computer. However, the effectiveness of these programs can vary depending on how long it's been since the file was deleted, how much the disk has been written to since, how fragmented the file was, what type of file system is used on the volume containing the file, and the size of the file.

If you need to recover deleted files, you should consider a standalone file recovery/undelete programs, such as

- **Recuva** —http://ethiopians.webs.com/downloads.htm
- **Recover My Files**—
  Http://www.soft82.com/download/Windows/Recover_My_Files

Recuva (pronounced "recover") is a freeware Windows utility to restore files that have been accidentally deleted from your computer. This includes files emptied from the recycle bin as well as images and other files that have been deleted by user error from digital camera memory cards or MP3 players. It will even bring back files that have been deleted by bugs, crashes and viruses!

Recover My Files enables recovering files which have been deleted in a permanent way from the rubbish bin, as well as files which have got lost due to the malicious activity of some virus, a software failure, or even files which may have got lost while formatting a partition.

Retrieving Data from Partitioned and Formatted Drives

When a hard disk, floppy disk, or removable-media drive containing files is formatted, the links and pointers to the clusters occupied by the existing files are lost. If a hard drive has been repartitioned or reformatted, the original file system and partition information are lost as well.

In such cases, more powerful data-recovery tools must be used to retrieve data. To retrieve data from an accidentally partitioned or formatted drive, you have a few options:

- Use a program that can unformat or unpartition the drive.
- Use a program that can bypass the newly created file system and read disk sectors directly to discover and retrieve data.

Recover data from a computer that will not boot

If Windows is corrupted and the system will not boot, recovering your data might be your first priority. One way to get to the data is to remove your hard drive from your computer and install it as a second non-booting hard drive in another system. After you boot up the system, you should be able to use Windows Explorer to copy the data to another medium. If the data is corrupted, try to use data recovery software. You can use IDE to USB converter kit or a SATA to USB converter to temporarily connect a desktop or notebook hard drive to a USB port on a working computer.

9.3. Review Questions

1. What is the difference between data backup and recovery?
2. What are the steps used to back up your files in window 7
3. How do you recover files within the recycle bin?
4. List some software tools used to recover deleted files in your computer?
5. How do you recover deleted data from a computer that will not boot?

Chapter Ten

Common Problems and Solutions

☞ **How can I speed up my PC? It has become very slow.**

There are a number of factors that can cause a computer to run slowly. Here are some of the basic reasons which may cause the computer to run slow.

- Unnecessary *Startup* Programs Running in the Background
- Not enough space on the hard disk
- Viruses
- Insufficient RAM
- Registry Issues

Customize Startup Programs:-Many of the programs and applications that you install on your PC start automatically each time that your computer boots up. In certain cases they will launch immediately after you login to Windows, and other times they may run silently in the background. Either way, these programs that are running can slow down your PC. Use **msconfig** to disable unneeded *startup* programs.

Not enough space on the hard disk:- Adding very bulky programs and files will automatically slow down your computer system. Users with a hard disk capacity of 2GB need to leave at least 250MB free, and those with a higher hard disk storage capacity need to leave at least 20% of the total capacity free. This will allow your computer enough room for both temporary files and file swapping.

To increase hard disk space apply the following actions

- Uninstall unneeded Programs
- Run Disk cleanup

- Defragment the hard disk

Viruses: - Adware, malware and spyware software can considerably reduce the computer performance. Of course the easy way out of this problem is to install antivirus software in your computer. But one thing that you need to keep in mind is that, antivirus software though a necessity can also reduce the performance of your computer. Hence, it becomes very important that you choose antivirus software, which does not occupy a lot of RAM.

Insufficient RAM: - The more RAM a computer has, the faster it will run. If you are using software which takes large amount of RAM, then obviously, the other applications will run slow. You should have enough RAM memory to process all the tasks at hand. If you don't, this can cause a major slowing of your computer while it is booting up or processing tasks.

Registry Issues: Over time, the registry can become cluttered with duplicate information, orphaned keys, or blank spaces. Improper shutdowns can be caused by power outages and impatient users; as a result, the windows registry can become corrupted. Any of these issues can cause windows registry errors that slow the system. Although users can manually change the registry using the regedit.exe utility, this solution is time intensive and risky. Instead, using a registry cleaner to automatically correct the information stored in the Windows registry is the best course of action. Using this program from time to time can help keep the registry clean and organized

☞ **Deep Freeze is installed on my computer. I would like to uninstall it. How is this done?**

Disable Deep Freeze before uninstalling it.

To disable Deep Freeze:

1. Hold down the shift key and double-click the Deep Freeze icon. Alternatively, you can press CTRL+ALT+SHIFT+F6.
2. Enter your password and click OK
3. If you have not yet entered a password you should be able to click OK without entering a password.
4. The Boot Options dialog is displayed. Select "Boot Thawed" and click OK. This will disable Deep Freeze on the next reboot.
5. **Reboot your computer. After the computer reboots, you are ready to** uninstall Deep Freeze.

To uninstall deep freeze:
1. Locate the installation file you used to install Deep Freeze on your computer. By default, the name of this file is called "DF5Std.exe" for versions 5.X and "DF6Std.exe" for versions 6.X.
2. Run the installation file (DF5Std.exe or DF6Std.exe).
3. Select the option to "Uninstall"

☞ **How to remove "window is not genuine' problem on window 7**

Windows 7 may sometimes been detected as illegal, not genuine, or Pirated despite the operating system has been genuinely bought from market. Then it shows a message "'**Activate Windows now**" immediately after log on. Moreover, the computer desktop background is turned to black, after some time of logging in and the error message "*This copy of Windows is not genuine* " is shown on the bottom right corner of the screen:

To solve this problem use either of the following methods

Method 1: Use command prompt
1. Click Start →All programs →Accessories
2. Right click command prompt and choose run as administrator

3. Now in the command prompt window, type **slmgr -rearm** and press enter

4. Restart your system. Try to restart your system twice.

Method 2: disable the plug and play policy

1. Determine the source of the policy. To do this, follow these steps:

2. On the client computer experiencing the activation error, run the **Resultant Set of Policy** wizard by clicking **Start >> Run** (or press Win+R keys), and entering **rsop.msc** as the command.

3. Visit the following location: **Computer Configuration -> Policies -> Windows Settings ->Security Settings -> System Services**

   • If the Plug and Play service is configured through a Group Policy setting, you see it here with settings other than **Not Defined**.

4. change the setting to "Not Defined"

5. Force the Group Policy setting to reapply: **gpupdate /force** (a restart of the client is sometimes required).

☞ **How to remove virus without antivirus software**

Removing virus without using antivirus program is possible but it can be risky task.A person can delete all virus from a computer or memory cards without using antivirus if you know which files are needed for operating system or application software and which are virus part. Here are two methods for removing virus

   • Command Prompt
   • Registry keys

✓ How to remove virus using command prompt

Each file and folder has the following attributes

- Archive A
- Read Only R
- Hidden H
- System S

- (minus) sign before an attribute it means removing attributes and + (plus) sign mean giving attributes to the file or folder. For example, **attrib *-r -a -s -h* file.txt this** will remove all attributes from file.txt and **attrib *+r +a +s +h* file.txt** *will* give all attributes to file.txt. If your hard drive is infected by virus, Command prompt is the best option. Follow the steps given below.

1. Go to the **command prompt** by start→all programs→ accessories→ **command prompt** or press windows key+r and enter cmd.
2. Go to the drive where you want to delete **virus** example write *d:* to go to D drive.
3. Type *attrib -r -s -h *.* /s /d* and press enter.
4. Press *dir /a*.
5. Delete all the .inf, .exe, .dll, .log extension file if they are not your files by using DOS Del command. Example Del *autorun.inf*

If any file is not deleting rename that file by *rename* command Example rename *dst.exe ms.bak* this will rename dst.exe to ms.bak. Now your drive is virus free.

✓ How to remove virus using Registry key

It's hard to remove the virus in the Windows System Registry, because it's not easy to find where the virus hides. Also, it's danger to edit the data inside the registry. If you enter or delete wrong key, data or value, windows might be unable to run after that. Here I just show you how to check any unwanted program loaded into the memory when windows start.

To change the registry data needs to run **Microsoft registry editor** - RegEdit.exe. You can click the **Start** Button, and then select **Run...** item. When the **Run** Window will appear, then type regedit textbox and click **ok** button.

You might be unable to **regedit**, because the virus blocks the doorway. In this case, you need to bring up your windows in **Safe Mode** to run the RegEdit. Sometimes, you need to login the Administrator account. Therefore, make sure you know your Administrator account's password when you own the new computer.

System Registry has **Run, RunOnce** and **RunOnceEx** entry nodes to manage which program can run while Windows is starting.

- First, you should check any starting programs inside the HEKY_LOCAL_MACHINE.

- Go down to the node in HEKY_LOCAL_MACHINE\SOFTWARE\Microsoft\Windows\CurrentVersion, then look for program entry inside the Run, RunOnce and RunOnceEX. If you find something you don't know, then you type the program name .exe name into the following Search box to find out what's that. If the .exe name is the virus or spyware, then you can delete it.   Google [   ] Search

- Go down to the node in HEKY_CURRENT_USER\SOFTWARE\Microsoft\Windows\Current

171

Version, and then look for unwanted .exe programs inside the Run, RunOnce and RunOnceEX. If you find something, then delete them.Some virus will restore the entry later or reboot; even you delete the entry from System Registry Editor. Those viruses need special tools to kill them.

☞ **How to enable windows task manager when disabled by a virus**

Even if you have anti-virus installed, you can still be infected by a new or custom virus that is not recognized by your anti-virus. Sometimes after removing the virus completely from our system, you'll face new problems such as you can no longer bring up Windows Task Manager from CTRL+ALT+DEL. You get the error message saying "Task Manager has been disabled by your administrator". Disabling Task Manager is one way viruses try to make it harder for you to deal with their infections. Before proceeding any further, you should run a complete and up-to-date anti-virus scan of your computer. It's possible, perhaps even likely, that you've been infected. Once you come back virus-free, you can proceed with the fix.

If you have Windows XP/7, Click **Start**, then click **Run** and type in **gpedit.msc** and press **OK.**

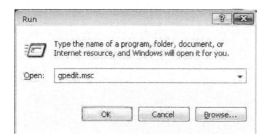

Figure 10.1 Opening group policy editor

Once in the Group Policy Editor, expand in turn:

- User Configuration
- Administrative Templates
- System
- Ctrl+Alt+Del Options

Double click on **Remove Task Manager** to change its setting. Click on **Not Configured** and then **OK** and Task Manager is available once again.

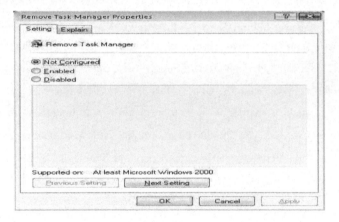

Figure 10.2 Configuring task managers

☞ **How to check power supply unit functionality using paper clip test**

There are various reasons why a computer will shut down. Chief among these is component overheating. The most common cause of computer overheating is a fan going bad and failing to cool down a component. When a PSU fan goes bad, it is not able to cool down the power supply hence the device will heat up. The excess heat generated by the PSU will add to the

173

overall temperature of the system unit. If this failure is not corrected, the PSU will become damage. A damaged PSU can, potentially, damage the components as well as the motherboard, itself. If your system appears to be exhibiting an, abnormally, high temperature and you suspect that the PSU's fan has gone bad but are not sure, there is a test you can perform which should prove whether the fan is working or not. This test is called, "The PSU Paper Clip Test."

To perform the PSU Paper Clip test, we'll need to examine the power supply connectors closely and find the one that has a lone green wire. In addition to the green wire, locate the other black wires that are present in the connector. Once the wires are located, you will need a paper clip.

Make sure that the power cord is **NOT** connected to the power supply then connect one end of the paper clip to the green wire and the other end to one of the black wires present on the connector as shown below:

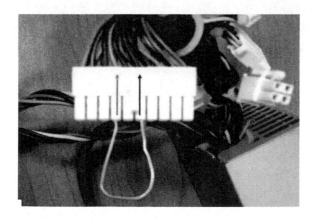

Figure 10.3   Green and black wires +paper clip

If the fan turns, then this means that the PSU is, at least, delivering some oltages out and overheating might not be occurring. If, on the other hand, the fan does not turn, then overheating is, most, likely occurring and the PSU will eventually fail and may damage some other components, in the process. This test works ninety nine percent of the time. There is, however, that one percent. If you want to be sure of the power supply's functionality I would suggest that you purchase a power supply tester. This will give you, more, accurate results then the PSU Paper Clip test.

☞ **A Computer with window 7 performs an automatic repair during start up and shuts down itself.**

To solve this problem, you can use startup Repair in window 7
Startup Repair is one of the recovery tools in the *System Recovery Options* menu. It allows you to fix certain system problems that might prevent Windows 7 from booting successfully. This utility is designed to fix only certain problems such as missing or damaged system files used to load the operating system. It can't detect or fix hardware failures nor does it help against virus attacks and their damage. When Windows 7 fails to boot properly, this utility automatically starts up and scans your PC for issues (like corrupt system files or an invalid boot file), then tries to fix the problem.

How to Use Startup Repair
Once you've accessed the *System Recovery* window, select *Startup Repair*.
The tool scans your computer for the problem and then tries to fix it so your computer can start correctly.

☞ How to create partition in window 7

Partitioning a hard drive in windows 7 has become a lot easier than in previous Windows versions because windows 7 is equipped with a Disk Management tool. With this tool you can partition your hard drive, shrink or expand volumes, and create new ones.

To launch the Disk Management tool

Start and type →**diskmgmt.msc** in the search box →press enter key
   Or

Right click on my computer →choose manage→on the left pane under storage click disk management.
   Or

Open control panel →administrative tools→computer management →disk management

Steps to create a new partition on your hard disk using Disk Management

1. Open disk management tool. In Disk Management's Graphical view, right-click an unallocated or free area, and then click New Simple Volume. This starts the New Simple Volume Wizard.
2. Read the Welcome page and then click next.
3. Size the partition in megabytes using the Simple Volume Size field and then click next.
4. On the Assign Drive Letter or Path page, specify whether you want to assign a drive letter or path and then click next.
5. Use the Format Partition page to determine whether and how the volume should be formatted.
6. Click next, confirm your options, and then click Finish.

To shrink a volume using disk management tool

To make unused disk space available, you can decrease the size of a volume by shrinking it - without having to format the disk.

The Steps are:

1. Right click the volume (drive letter) you want to shrink
2. Click shrink volume …
3. Follow the instructions on your screen

☞ **How to remove one of the operating system in a dual boot**

Depending on the size of your hard drive, you can have several different partitions on your hard drive. Each of these partitions can have different operating systems that can be booted--that is, used to start up and run your computer. Removing one of these operating systems, including Windows 7, from a dual-boot system can be done from inside any windows-based operating system.

If you want hide an operating system from dual or triple boot, follow these steps:

1. Right click on **My Computer** and select **properties**
2. Move to the **advanced** tab
3. Under **Startup and Recovery** select **Settings**
4. In startup and recovery window, under system startup select the operating system that you don't want to hide
5. Uncheck 'time to display list of operating systems'
6. Click **ok** twice, then reboot. You should go directly to your preferred operating system

☞ **How to properly delete window Vista in a Dual Boot**

1. Boot up a non-Vista partition that has a Windows OS installed.

2. Open control panel

3. Open the "Administrative Tools" menu

4. Double-click the "Computer Management" icon to open a new window

5. Select "Disk Management," located under the "Storage" menu option, to open a list of drives and partitions on each drive

6. Right-click the drive partition that contains Windows Vista.

7. Click "Format" from the menu that appears when you right-click the partition. This will delete Windows Vista from the hard drive and format the free space to work on your current OS. Once the partition is formatted (a process that will take several minutes), the extra space will be ready to use on your current partition, and Vista will no longer appear on a list of bootable operating systems when your PC starts.

☞ **Enable or disable secure logon in window 7**

It's important to keep your computer as secure as possible. One way to do this is to enable secure logon, which requires you to press Ctrl+Alt+Delete to log on.

Steps

1. Open run by Press widow +R

2. Type **control userpasswords2** in the test box

3. Click the Advanced tab, select the require users to press Ctrl+Alt+Delete check box, and then click OK.

To change the desktop background/wallpaper in window 7

1. Open control panel→personalization→click on the Desktop Background at the bottom of the opened window.

2. Click the picture or color that you want to use for your desktop background. If the picture you want to use isn't in the list of desktop background pictures, click an item in the Picture location list to see other categories, or click Browse to search for the picture on your computer. When you find the picture that you want, double-click it. It will become your desktop background.

☞ **Power geez icon missing from notification area in windows XP**

After a computer started, one or more icons are missing and disappearing from the task bar notification area. The exact cause for the problem is unknown. Sometimes virus is the most common cause for this problem. There are different solutions for this problem. If you face this problem, try the following solutions.

Solution 1: disable SSDP Discovery Service

1. Right-click My Computer, and then click Manage.

2. Click Services and Applications.

3. Double-click Services.

4. In the Services list, right-click SSDP Discovery Service, and then click Properties.

5. On the General tab, in the Startup type drop-down list, click Disabled.

6. Click OK.

Solution 2: Use secure login

1. Click on Start

2. Click on Run.

3. Type "control userpasswords2".

4. Click OK

5. Check (Select) Users must enter a user name and password to use this computer.

6. Click OK

Solution 3: Install window XP

If the above solution doesn't work, you can install windows XP using repair installation or clean installation.

Solution 4: Install window 7

Sometimes installing windows XP doesn't solve the problem. So, you will be forced to change the operating system. Installing windows 7 will finally solve the problem.

☞ **How to remove the error message "There is no disk in the drive".**
Please insert a disk into drive \device\hard disk2\DR2

Solution 1:

Use windows task manager to kill the process.

To open task manager use combination of keys Ctrl +Alt+Del.

Solution2:

Use registry

Start→regedit→HKEY_LOCAL_MACHINE→system→controlset→cont rol→windows→on the right pane click →error mode→change the value from 0 to 2.

☞ My laptop suddenly changes to Black screen

Situation 1:

When you plug the AC adapter the power LED and the battery charge LED light up. When you press on the power button the laptop will not start and you cannot hear any activity from the hard drive, cooling fan and the DVD drive.

Unplug the AC adapter, remove the battery and wait for 1-2 minutes. After that plug the AC adapter and try starting the laptop again. Sometimes this trick helps. It also could be a **memory related problem**. Try reseating the memory module, just remove it from the slot on the motherboard and install it back. Try installing the memory module into the other slot (if it's available). If you have two memory modules installed, try removing them one by one and start the laptop just with one memory module installed.

Situation 2:

The laptop appears to be dead. You plug the AC adapter but the LEDs (power light, hard drive light, battery charge light, etc…) do not light up and the laptop will not react at all if you press on the power button.

First of all in this situation check the AC adapter. You can test the output voltage with a voltmeter. If you cannot do that, find a known good AC adapter and use it for testing the laptop. It is possible the laptop appears to be dead because the AC adapter is bad (and the battery is discharged). If you know that the AC adapter is working properly and it outputs correct voltage but the laptop is still dead, most likely you have a power issue on the motherboard (or power board on some laptops) and it has to be replaced.

If you have to replace the AC adapter, make sure you use a correct one. The output voltage must be exactly the same as on the original adapter. The output amperage has to be the same as on the original adapter or higher, but not lower.

☞ Laptop backlight and Inverter problems

The symptoms are that the laptop display panel will flicker and then appear to switch off, but if you look closely you can still see a very faint image on the panel, almost like peering through the dark, this is because the backlight isn't lit. Inverter boards have been an issue in a lot of makes and models of laptops – this is a very common fault. The inverter board loses proper connection causing the backlight to flicker or just simply fails altogether.

A little info in what we mean when we say 'Back Light'. Your screen has a fluorescent tube inside it which is just like your normal household tube except for its size, it's about 1/10 of the size. The tube is attached to a small circuit board via a cable, the circuit board acts like the starter in your household variety. This circuit board is called an 'Inverter or FL Inverter'; the inverter provides regulated power to the fluorescent tube which lights up the screen. If the Inverter fails then you appear to have no display, yes and no, the screen is still displaying the image but without light from the tube it only appears ever so faintly.

☞ Can't format my laptop with window XP which was window 7 installed previously

Most Laptops come with window 7 or vista installed. But when you try to install/format the laptop with window XP, the installation will not work properly. This means that if you are installing Windows XP on a system with a SATA host adapter set to AHCI or RAID mode and Windows XP does not recognize the drive, you will need to press the F6 key and install the

AHCI/RAID drivers. In this case, changing the host adapter from AHCI to IDE mode allows you to install windows XP properly.

To set the hard disk host adapter to IDE in BIOS

1. Enter CMOS set up
2. Set the hard disk AHCI mode to IDE or SATA or legacy mode.
3. Save the configuration and exit from BIOS

☞ **How to Enable the (Hidden) Administrator Account on Windows 7 or Vista**

Method 1:

1. Open a command prompt in administrator mode by right-clicking and choosing "Run as administrator"
2. Type the following command: net user administrator /active:yes
3. You should see a message that the command completed successfully. Log out, and you'll now see the Administrator account as a choice.

Method 2:

Control panel→administrative tools→computer management →local users and groups→users→Right click on the administrative account→choose properties→on general tab→uncheck 'account is disable'

☞ **How to disable Built-in Administrator Account**

1. Open an administrator mode command prompt as above. Type the following command: net user administrator /active:no
2. The administrator account will now be disabled, and shouldn't show up on the login screen anymore.

☞ I start the laptop and it starts making repetitive clicking noise or grinding noise

Most likely you hear this noise because of a faulty hard drive. You can remove the hard drive and start the laptop without it. If the noise is gone, the hard drive is your problem. Replace it.

If the laptop makes clicking or grinding noises and you still have video on the screen, you can run a hard drive test utility. You can use hard drive test utilities such as Hitachi's drive fitness test. This test is reliable and easy to use.

☞ CD-ROM drive disappeared and I cannot see it in My Computer window. What can I do?

Sometimes you may not see the CD-ROM or the DVD-ROM drive in the My Computer window. This problem is very common for laptop and might be caused by a failed drive or by corrupted software. You can try the following repair steps before you decide that your drive is bad.

- Try checking the drive functionality in the device manager
- You can try to reseat the optical drive. Overtime the CD-ROM drive connector might get oxidized and a simple drive reseating can fix the problem. Try to remove the drive from the laptop and put it back. See if it will fix the problem.
- You can also try to boot from any bootable CD to see if you laptop recognize the CD-ROM drive on BIOS level. Put any bootable CD (Live Linux CD, Windows XP CD, Windows 2000 CD, etc) into the CD-ROM drive and change the boot order to start from the CD-ROM drive. If you laptop starts to boot from the CD, then the drive is recognized in BIOS and most likely it operates properly. In this case

look for a software problem. It might be necessary to reload the operating system to fix the software problem. If you cannot boot your laptop from a bootalbe CD, then the drive might be bad itself.

☞ The power button won't turn off the system

Most recent laptop systems are configured to shut down automatically when you exit Windows. However, you sometimes need to shut down the system manually. There are several possible reasons why the power button might not shut down the system. Check the following before you consider sending the system in for service:

- Power-management problems some systems might not implement power management properly. Make sure the system is set to shut down when you push the power button; some systems might be configured to go into a sleep mode instead.
- Buggy system BIOS Reflash the BIOS with a different version. If you are using the most recent BIOS version, go back to the previous version if possible.

☞ The system won't shut down in Windows

Windows should startup and shutdown like turning a light switch on and off. But sometimes instead of shutting down, Windows XP may reboot. So the first thing we need to do is disabling Windows "restart on system failure" feature.

Select *Start →Control Panel* to open the Control Panel. In the Control Panel select *Performance and Maintenance* → *System* to open the *System Properties* dialog box. In the *System Properties* dialog box, select the Advanced tab and in the *Startup and Recovery* section, click on the Settings button

In the Startup and Recovery dialog box that appears, in the *System Failure* section, uncheck the box next to "Automatically restart". Then click on the OK button.

Below is a list of possible causes for Windows XP to fail to shut down:

- A Virus or Spyware is Preventing Shutdown
- A Software Application is Preventing Shutdown
- A program Loaded at Startup is Preventing Shutdown
- A Hardware Device is Preventing Shutdown
- Advanced Power Management (APM) is Preventing Shutdown

☞ A Virus or Spyware is Preventing Shutdown

A Virus or spyware application may preventing your computer from shutting down while it attempts to use your internet connection to communicate the personal information that it gathered from your computer to it's creator.

☞ A Software Application is Preventing Shutdown

A software application may prevent Windows from shutting down. This usually occurs the first time you try shutting down Windows after installing a new software application, but can also occur if a shared module changes or has been corrupted. You may need to uninstall software applications one at a time to determine which one may be preventing shutdown.

☞ A Hardware Device is Preventing Shutdown

A hardware device can prevent Windows from shutting down. This usually occurs the first time you try shutting down Windows after installing a new hardware device, but can also occur after a configuration change or if a hardware driver has been corrupted.

☞ A program Loaded at Startup is Preventing Shutdown

A program run by Windows When it starts may prevent Windows from shutting down. Use *MSConfig command* to selectively disable these programs at startup or manually close them down before you shut down the computer.

☞ Advanced Power Management (APM) is Preventing Shutdown

APM controls the power saving features of your computer. Power saving features is important with a battery powered system, however APM is a common source of problems, so if your system is constantly plugged into an AC outlet, it may be best to disable APM.

The most frequent problem with APM is the computer goes into standby mode or hibernation and can't come out of it.

With a battery powered system, disabling APM can eliminate it as a cause of shutdown problems. Select *Start →Control Panel* to open the *Control Panel*. In *Control Panel* select *Performance and Maintenance → Power Options* to open the *Power Options Properties* dialog box. In the *Power Options Properties* dialog box select the APM tab and uncheck the box next to "Enable Advanced Power Management support".

☞ Can I run 32-bit applications on 64-bit computer?

Most programs designed for the 32-bit version of windows will work on the 64-bit version of Windows. Notable exceptions are many antivirus programs. Device drivers designed for the 32-bit version of Windows don't work on computers running a 64-bit version of Windows. If you're trying to install a printer or other device that only has 32-bit drivers available, it won't work correctly on a 64-bit version of Windows.

If the program is specifically designed for the 64-bit version of Windows, it won't work on the 32-bit version of Windows.

☞ "My laptop is unable to boot" and it has to be formatted. How can I back up my files before formatting?

If your laptop is unable to boot, the first work you have to do is repair installation. If repairing doesn't solve, you can format your laptop. But before you do formatting; you have to back up your existing files and programs. Below are some of the methods to protect and back up your files before formatting.

1. If you have two partitions (say C and D), check whether your files are in partition D and the operating system is in partition C. if your important files are in drive D and the operating system is in drive C, formatting drive C will not delete your files.

2. **Hiren's BootCD** can help you to back up your files before installing operating systems.

3. **Ubuntu live CD** -- you can use an Ubuntu Live CD to back up and recover data

4. Remove the hard disk from the laptop and connect the laptop hard drive to the desktop computer. This will be possible if laptop hard drive interface is compatible to the desktop hard drive interface. You may configure the desktop hard disk as master and the laptop hard disk as slave. So that you can to back up your data.

☞ How to Disable AutoPlay feature to prevent Virus spreading using this feature.

Cause: Most of the Malware and worm uses auto run feature of windows to Spread & launch to your machine.

Solution:

- Go to Start and Run
- Type gpedit.msc
- Click Ok
- This will open a new group policy window.
- In the group policy window click on the plus sign next to Administrative Templates under Computer configuration.
- Then Click on system & then you will find turn off Autoplay on the right-hand side.
- Double click on the Turn off Autoplay. It will open a new window
- By default it will set to Not configured.
- Select Enable & select it for all drive then click Apply and OK.
- Close the Group Policy Window.

☞ **How can I practice installing windows XP without   deleting my files and programs?**

You can practice installing operating systems (like window XP, window 7, and window vista) without affecting your existing programs and files using virtual machine software. A **virtual machine** (**VM**) is a "completely isolated guest operating system installation within a normal host operating system. It is a separate and independent software instance that includes a full copy of an operating system and application software. For example, if you have a computer with window XP, you can install window 7 on window XP virtually. To do this you must have virtual machine software like oracle virtual box to be installed on window XP and window 7 image file.

☞ Can I install window 7 using USB flash disk?

You can install window 7 using USB devices by creating a bootable Windows 7 USB flash drive. You may get the steps for creating bootable window 7 USB flash on the internet.

☞ When I write a text on Microsoft Word I can't change font style permanently and the automatic spelling checker doesn't work when writing English texts.

Solution: the input language may be set as Amharic, so try correcting the input language into English (United States) using the following steps:-

Control panel→region and language→keyboard and language tab→change keyboard→general tab→choose English (United States)-US

☞ My laptop installed with a language other than English and I can't do anything on it?

Solution:

1. Please try the option to choose English and read the manuals that come with the laptop.
2. If the first option fails, install windows 7 from scratch that support the language you prefer.

☞ After boot up my laptop by pressing the power button, the windows logon screen doesn't appear and I can't log into my PC.

Solution: there are many causes for this problem, but the most common cause for the problem is being infected with virus.

Try the following methods to solve the problem:-

1. Login to your computer with safe mode by pressing F8
2. After login with safe mode, you can create a new user account.

3. Use the new account for your next login

4. You may delete the old user account if you don't need it

5. if the above steps doesn't work , repair your computer

☞ **While I am copying any file I get this error "file integrity violated"**

How to Fix this Error?

- Try to remove/reinstall any installed program of fast copy software such as Tera copy

- If that program still not uninstall then use any third party uninstalling software

☞ **Folders and documents hidden by virus**

When you open Documents or Pictures and see nothing there, your files are just hidden. This does not mean that they are deleted rather a virus has hidden the folder. To unhide your folders and documents you may follow the following steps for window 7 professional.

1. Open the drive or folder where your files and folders are hidden

2. On the left hand corner of the opened window, click on 'organize' then choose "folder and search options"

3. On the folder options dialog box , click on view tab

4. Under advanced settings, click show hidden files, folders, and drives, and then uncheck "hide protected operating systems files"

5. Click OK

☞ **Windows says that I am running out of disk space**

- This alert will appear when a hard drive is running very low on free space. The error flags relative to the size of the disk, so larger drives will have more free space remaining when this error appears.

- **Solution:** Windows XP users should run *cleanmgr* from the Run menu while Windows7 users should do a Windows Search for Disk Cleanup. This will pull up a utility that can purge a hard drive of unneeded files like temporary files and files stuck in the recycle bin.

☞ **Files open, but nonsense characters appear**

Check and/or Try the following

- The program used to open the file is not the correct program for that type of file. For example, a Microsoft Word file opened in Notepad will show nonsense characters.

- The file could be corrupted. Check the hard drive for damage and scan the system for viruses and malware.

☞ **Windows says my computer isn't secure**

- Microsoft has given Windows built-in security alerts that flag if your computer isn't protected by antivirus software. This triggers a pop-up alert originating in the system tray

- *Solution*: Open the Windows Action Center, which can be found in the Control Panel. This will tell you what is causing the security alert to show up. In most cases, the problem is a lack of anti-malware software on your PC. This problem can easily be solved by downloading Microsoft Security Essentials.

☞ Windows does not detect all of the RAM I have installed

- This issue, which can be a problem with computers that have four gigabytes of Random Access Memory (RAM) or more, is evident in the System window. Instead of listing the proper amount of RAM, Windows will list that some smaller amount is installed, most likely a number between three and four gigabytes.

- *Solution:* In the System window, find the information field labeled System type. It will likely say"32-bit Operating System." To address four gigabytes of RAM or more, you must have Windows64-bit installed. You will need to re-install Windows with a 64-bit installation disk to resolve the problem

☞ My USB device isn't working

- USB is plug-and-play, which means that a USB device should work automatically. However, in rare instances a USB device will not be detected

- *Solution:* First make sure that the USB device is plugged into the correct USB port. Old computers will have USB 1.1 ports, which might not function right with all modern USB devices. If using a USB hub, try plugging the device into your PC directly rather than via the hub. Some USB devices need to draw power from the port to function and a hub may not provide enough or any power.

- If these solutions still don't resolve the issue, the problem is likely related to the USB device's drivers. Go to the device manufacturer's website and download any drivers that the company has made available, then reboot your computer and try your device again.

References

1. Minasi, Mark. The complete PC upgrade and maintenance guide. SYBEX Inc., 1997.

2. Michael W. Graves. A+ guide to pc hardware maintenance and repair. Vol. 1. Cengage Learning, 2004.

3. Brooks, Charles J. CompTIA A+ Exam Cram (Exams 220-602, 220-603, 220-604)(Exam Cram). Que Corp., 2007.

4. "Window 7 installation guide". URL: http://getintopc.com/tutorials/how-to-install-windows-7-step-by-step-method-for-beginners/

5. Hardware troubleshooting. URL: http://www.pcbuyerbeware.co.uk/MotherboardProblems.htm

6. Scott Mueller, Brian Knittel." Upgrading and Repairing Microsoft Windows",Que publisher, November 30, 2005

7. Victor Rudometov and Evgeny. "PC Overclocking, Optimization & Tuning, Second Edition", A-LIST Publishing,2002.

8. Joel Rosenthal and Kevin Irwin. "PC Repair and Maintenance: A Practical Guide", Charles River Media,2004.

9. Ron Gilster. "A+ Certification For Dummies", Hungry Minds publishing Inc,2001

Printed in Great Britain
by Amazon

19018858R00119